I AM JUSTICE

PAUL KENYON is an award-winning journalist who has
work   the BBC for almost twenty years. He is currently
a rep   *Panorama*, and it was whilst making a two-
part do   entary on African migrants in 2007 that he
became friends with Justice Amin.

I Am Justice
A Journey Out of Africa

Paul Kenyon

preface
publishing

This paperback edition published by Preface 2010

10 9 8 7 6 5 4 3 2 1

First published in Great Britain in 2009 by Preface Publishing
20 Vauxhall Bridge Road
London SW1V 2SA

An imprint of The Random House Group

www.rbooks.co.uk
www.prefacepublishing.co.uk

Addresses for companies within The Random House Group Limited
can be found at www.randomhouse.co.uk

The Random House Group Limited Reg. No. 954009

A CIP catalogue record for this book is available from the British Library

ISBN 978 1 84809 148 1

Mixed Sources
Product group from well-managed
forests and other controlled sources
www.fsc.org Cert no. TT-COC-2139
© 1996 Forest Stewardship Council

The Random House Group Limited supports The Forest Stewardship Council (FSC), the leading international forest certification organisation. All our titles that are printed on Greenpeace-approved FSC-certified paper carry the FSC logo. Our paper procurement policy can be found at www.rbooks.co.uk/environment

Typeset in Palatino by Palimpsest Book Production Limited,
Grangemouth, Stirlingshire

Printed and bound in Great Britain by CPI Bookmarque, Croydon CR0 4TD

Both lands had once been part of the same. There was sand and rock still fresh from the stars, and a salt desert which writhed and folded and threw fire into the sky. And the desert formed a basin, and beyond the basin to the west was a raging ocean which burst through in a mighty waterfall and poured an entire ocean into the space it found. Then explorers crossed the water, followed by armies. There were battles fought and great ships lost, and conquerors crowned as kings. And the men of the north took all that was good from the land across the sea, all that was laced into the earth, or ripening beneath the hot sun. And when they returned to the north, with all that they could carry, some of those from whom they'd taken decided to follow . . .

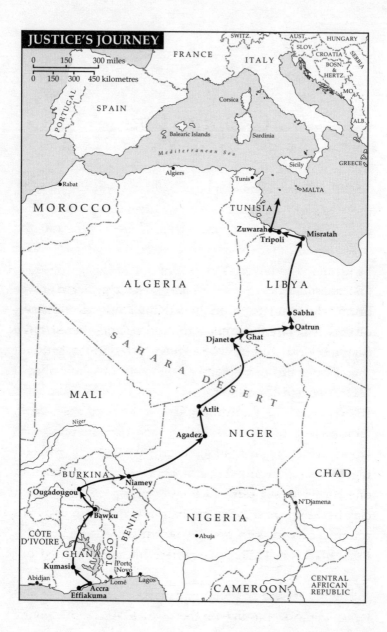

Chapter One

Justice Amin heard his uncle patting on the goatskin dondo drum. He could taste the boiled tree bark, as the smell drifted in from the cauldron. 'Today uncle must have customers,' he said to Issah, lying beside him on the mat. 'I will leave before he starts.'

He pulled a pair of trousers from a nail on the wall and waited behind the door. On the other side was a dark, windowless porch. It was hammered from planks of wood, which were weathered and broken and patched together so unevenly that the whole structure leaned. In one corner was a piece of board, on top of which sat a clay head. It was smooth and hairless, its mouth and eyes roughly carved with a stick. Down its sides dripped a thick black crust. This was where his uncle carried out the sacrifices.

The hut looked out onto a main road where buses and lorries rumbled through on their way to Accra, five hours' drive east. They didn't bother stopping in the small community of Effiakuma. The fresh tarmac with its clean white lines and straight borders was the most orderly, well-designed feature in town. The only other roads were dust tracks, lined with abandoned mountains of cement and gravel, and pitted with holes so large they could swallow a car.

On either side of the road were sloping tin roofs which stretched away to the forest. They were corrugated, bronzed by monsoon, and covered in large boulders which had been carefully positioned to stop them flying off in the wind. The buildings were mostly breeze block smeared with cement. The older ones were made from wood. Some were painted with bright murals, advertising Coca-Cola or Anchor butter. 'Reach for Greatness' read one, and then underneath in black letters, 'Guinness'.

Many of the roadside properties doubled as shops: 'Nina's wigs', 'Mabe's flour', 'Madam Odobu's herbal centre'. Inside there was usually a single windowless room with the wares spread out on the floor. One, called 'John's Honourable Venture', was a bare wooden hut which opened directly onto the main road. Inside John sat at a small table, a typewriter in front of him, composing letters for the illiterate of Effiakuma.

Passing beneath the road, and weaving its way between the shacks, was an open sewer. It was deeper than a child and too wide to leap. Narrow wooden planks bridged the gap, allowing residents to pass across in single file. Along its middle ran a continuous stream of liquids. To each side lay discarded clothes, plastic bags and bottles around which the solids gathered and baked in the sun.

Justice's hut was sandwiched between the main road and the communal washhouse. He lived with his uncle Ibrahim, his brother Issah who was three years his junior, and Zuleyha his baby sister. Beyond the leaning porch was a single room, where they ate, slept, and carried out any job their uncle demanded. The floor was clay, smoothed by years of bare feet, the walls grey brick. The only furniture was a wooden chair, a knee-high table, and a single bed. The children slept on mats. The bed was for the uncle.

Justice had lived with his uncle Ibrahim since he was five, maybe six years old. He wasn't sure. He never spoke of what went before, of his parents or what had happened. Neither did his uncle. The neighbours knew only that Justice's father had been a devout Muslim who studied the Koran and sometimes preached, and that he had lived with Justice's mother in the orange city of Agadez, on the edge of the Sahara in Niger. That was all. One day the three children arrived on a bus, with nothing more than a bag of clothes. They had lived with their uncle Ibrahim ever since.

For the first few years, there appeared to be harmony, despite the cramped conditions. It was when Justice reached his teenage years that the relationship with his uncle soured. 'Neither can finish a sentence without making the other one shout,' the neighbours would say. 'Maybe the boy's discovered the nature of his uncle's business.'

Separating the living area from the porch was a heavy wooden door. Its surface was covered in words. Some were scrawled wild and tall, with flourishes of white chalk, others were small and tidy, and curved down the edge of the frame to finish the thought. One read, 'The evil that man does lives after him.'

The drumming stopped. Justice heard Uncle Ibrahim tap a stick on the side of the cauldron, take a knife from the porch, and set off towards the forest. Then he slipped out, past the mosque and the lotto booth, pausing to queue at the thin wooden plank across the sewer which was livid with flies. The path narrowed. Goats rummaged and women kneaded clothes in giant tubs. He raced down an alleyway, geese and chickens flying from under his feet, past the smouldering rubbish tip, out onto the other side, and finally into a quieter area where there was a church tower made from slatted wood. Beneath it, on the other side of a sandy square was the Reverend Grant Methodist School.

'Little strong man,' a voice shouted from the balcony. 'Why do your legs move so quickly around a football, but turn to stone on the way to school?'

Justice slowed and walked the last few metres across the sand, taking care to show he was in no hurry. The school occupied the first floor of a narrow brick building, four classrooms long, and one deep. There was no glass in the windows, just slatted wooden shutters, which spent much of the year wide open so any movement of air could pass straight through. Most of the time, the rooms were still and humid, and smelt of damp clothes.

At the bottom of the steps he heard the voice again. It was gently chastising, but with an edge of humour which Justice had only recently learned to recognise. 'Little strong man, I don't suppose you're here for my lesson, are you?'

At the top of the first flight, was a concrete landing where the steps doubled back on themselves and rose to the stone balcony which ran the length of the building. The wall on the right of the stairwell carried verses from the Bible written in chalk, and above them in capitals, the words 'SPEAK ENGLISH ALWAYS'. Waiting at the top was the diminutive figure of Mr Ashie, the social studies teacher, slouching against the wall like he was waiting for a train.

'So, what now? Too early for technical drawing,' he frowned. 'But just in time for me.' He flourished a hand in front of Justice as if he was inviting in royalty and pushed open the classroom door. 'I've found a stranger,' he announced, and Justice walked in, head bowed, trying to hide his beaming smile.

There were sixty children in the class. The desks were wooden and varnished with countless years of sweat and grime, the walls lime green with a buttery texture up to shoulder height. In the rafters were two strip lights, required only in the rainy season when the skies darkened and the shutters were closed.

'When the British came to Ghana, they found gold in the earth and on the beaches . . .' Mr Ashie spoke English as well as the men on television, his arms drawing exuberant circles in the air. '. . . And there was so much of it, they called our land the Gold Coast, and they came here in their thousands. When they landed their boats, our people hid behind trees, but gradually the British lured them out with precious objects filled with magical properties. They were flat like water and thin as a child's finger; when they flashed them in our faces, anyone who dared look into them saw their own features staring back. And the British carried these things with them wherever they went and sometimes they used them to catch the sun and throw its light into dark corners.' Mr Ashie wrote some dates on the blackboard and then repositioned himself next to the map on the wall. Britain had been worn to a smudge, but he traced his finger around Spain, down past Senegal, Sierra Leone and Liberia to show the route the British took.

'Our ancestors were intrigued by these magical objects and asked if they could have some for their own. The British considered their request, and then announced their decision. "You can take these", they said, "if we can take the gold-coloured stones you have on your beaches and in your earth."'

Justice had heard similar stories before. One told of the cavernous cellars built beneath London and New York, to house all the African trees felled during British rule. They were treated with chemicals to keep them fresh; a secret stash of stolen hardwood that would last for centuries. Justice was embarrassed that his ancestors had been so compliant. He wasn't sure how it all ended, but understood that Britain and Ghana were still bound closely together.

He was sharing a desk with another boy, trying to copy shapes from the blackboard, when he heard a commotion outside. It was coming from the balcony near the headmaster's office. He recognised the voice.

'Ignore what you hear,' instructed the teacher. 'Mr Ashie is dealing with it.'

They carried on drawing for a while, but the voices came closer. Then the door was thrown open and in marched a short breathless man, unshaven, shoeless, and with dust falling from his hair. He was dressed in filthy shorts with a vest that appeared to be stained with blood.

'I want to see you,' the man shouted.

Justice was the only one in class who didn't look up.

'Now! You know you are needed.'

'I'm learning,' said Justice, still pushing his pencil around the page. 'Let me finish my class.'

Mr Ashie stood in the doorway, but didn't attempt to restrain the man. He'd disrupted classes before. The teachers knew he wouldn't leave until he got his way.

'I need you to go to the Numun tree,' the man persisted. 'There are customers waiting.'

He was losing patience and began weaving his way between the desks, towards the rear of the room where Justice was sitting.

'If you want him,' said the design teacher hurriedly, 'then the boy should walk out.' He was following the man now. 'Justice, if your uncle needs you, then you must follow his wish.'

His uncle stopped. Justice continued shading with a coloured pencil. He could smell the sweat and burning charcoal, and see the bare blackened feet to one side of his desk. He could smell his uncle's mouth.

'Let's go,' then his uncle poked him in the shoulder.

It was like a button had been pressed. Justice leapt to his feet so that the desk scraped noisily against the cement floor, shouldered his uncle out of the way, and charged for the door. He swung left at the walkway, past the headmaster's office, and came to a stop at the top of the concrete steps.

Uncle Ibrahim was following. 'I don't know why you

come here . . . these people, they teach you so many lies. What does their god know? Have they told you he will help you? Have they? Their god isn't a living god, he can do nothing for you. They tell you these lies to stop you finding the truth . . .'

Justice crouched in a ball at the top of the steps, his toes hanging over the edge. The only light in the stairwell came from the missing bricks, which threw patterns on the floor. Below, he could hear the shouts of the boys playing football in the dust. Behind him, the approaching footsteps of his uncle.

'You will not come here again. You don't need this place. You already have a job.'

Justice launched himself into the air: ten, fifteen steps he cleared, before he came crashing down on the concrete landing. The pain shot through his feet as if it were electric. There was a wall in front of him. He hit it hard, ricocheted to one side and landed full on his back, his head smacking the floor.

He was still for a moment and then tried to move. There was some pain, but it was fading fast. Nothing long lasting. He should have jumped higher, and hit the wall in mid-flight. That way, there would have been broken bones.

'Look at you,' came a voice from above. 'You behave like an animal. You have no shame. Get up and leave these people alone. We have customers today.'

Justice was a truant. That's how his teachers saw him. On the rare occasions he turned up, he showed some promise but was always too far behind to catch up. He had a quick mind but did little in the way of reading. His favourite lesson was technical drawing: towers, bridges, the local mosque,

he even did the homework. But he was fiery and unpredictable; arguing with the teachers one moment, idolising
them the next; truculent and sullen in the morning, sunshine
and charm in the afternoon. When the anger came, it was
often from a sense of offended morality. One day he saw a
boy stealing. He approached him outside school, asked him
why he'd been a thief, and then punched him to the ground.

When his uncle kept him from classes, he was often sent
to the rainforest, about half a mile from the hut. It was cool
under the canopy, and every now and then, when there
was a gap in the trees and the sun broke through, he would
stop to breathe in the aroma of baking leaves. There was
no path, just a trail of flattened undergrowth weaving
deeper into the bush.

He would stop first at the Neem tree, draw his machete,
and lop off a slice of bark which he'd place in a sack. The
ground was always scattered with seeds, which he'd also
collect. Over the years he'd compiled a notebook of every
plant and shrub his uncle required. 'Neem: boil leaves and
mix with bark. Cures: malaria.'

At the Guava tree, the rotting fruit attracted flies, not the
sort that bumble idly around but those as fierce as freshly-
shaved bees. Justice would hack a piece of root from the knots
around its base. 'Guava: chop roots and leaves, and then boil.
Cures: stomach complaints, diarrhoea. Also cleans the blood.'

He'd drawn pictures of some of them in pencil, separating
out the leaves, the fruit and the roots. When his brother
Issah was old enough, he'd be able to consult it. Some of
the plants he knew so well, he recognised them by smell
alone. The Nunum tree was the simplest, it smelt like the

ghosts of ancestors. 'Nunum: boil it, dry it, grind it. Many uses. Cut into skin to keep away danger.'

Often he would stay in the forest until the light flies flashed lime green and the smoke from Effiakuma's burning rubbish dump drifted through the trees on the night air.

One evening, Justice arrived home late and could see an amber glow through the gaps in the wooden porch. His uncle still had a customer. There would be candles laid out, he'd be pouring and mixing, spreading paste onto leaves, grinding cola nuts. The knife would be out. Justice dropped the sack of ingredients over the half-door and headed for the home of his best friend, Abu Bakia.

'When I am in my uncle's home,' he said, 'it is like the spirits are stepping on me.' He was lying near to Bakia, whose mother had provided sheets to keep the mosquitoes away. 'During the day, when he's not there, I can breathe. But at night, when I'm sleeping near to him, there are more than just four people in that room.'

Bakia's house was the most impressive in the district, two storeys high, and containing ten rooms or more, although it had never quite been finished. Metal stakes protruded from partially cemented walls, and wooden scaffolding had been jammed along its side for as long as Justice could remember. The house had an interior courtyard open to the stars, from which led uneven steps upwards and downwards, crumbling arches and dark tunnels. Then there were the walkways. They circled high above the courtyard, resting on precarious pillars, hung with clothing, pots and pans, prayer mats, shoes and kettles. Children hurtled through the corridors, chickens pecked the earth floor, women prepared fires which laced the entire building with the smell of burning wood. Over all this chaos presided the voluminous figure of Abu Bakia's father, a man held in high regard for the pilgrimage he'd made to Mecca when he was a young man doing well in the world. As with anyone who'd travelled to the Haj, they now called him 'Alhaji', a term of respect.

Alhaji had produced a village-worth of children: thirty from four wives. It was into this community that Justice would regularly retreat, either simply to sleep, or to find food. There were no set meals in his uncle's world and Justice was often left to scavenge whatever he could from friends and neighbours.

'My father remembers when your uncle used to attend the mosque,' said Bakia. 'They'd return here and the two of them would sit on the veranda and play chequers. They never see each other anymore.'

'He never sees anyone,' said Justice. 'Only customers.'

Bakia was a motorcycle repair man. It was just about the most exciting job in Effiakuma. His workshop was a shed beside the main road. It crackled and hummed with machinery and humanity, and was lit intermittently with plumes of fire which spread an amber mist across the unlit road. The real treat was that Bakia got to test drive whatever he'd mended. Sometimes for several days. Usually it was just a scooter but on occasions it would be a Kawasaki or a Yamaha and he would take off down the road, maybe as far as the beach, wearing shorts and a vest, slowing at Madam Molly's where he would wave to the girls mixing banku.

From as young as thirteen, Justice would ride pillion. The pair would take off to Takoradi, through the lush landscape, where the huts were hidden among the palms and mango trees, and where the girls would wave down traffic to offer smoked fish or spiced chicken from the circular boards balanced on their heads. It was about five miles to the stadium at Takoradi, and when they arrived Bakia would leave the bike with a friend. He and Justice would walk the final stretch, carried along by the crowds, slogans drawn across their bare chests in flour and water, banging drums and chanting.

They had decided not to support the local team. After much consideration they'd chosen Kotoko, from the rainforest region of central Ghana. 'They run like they are on fire,' said Justice, and the pair sat as close as they could to the front, sipping Coca-Cola and singing loudly with the visitors.

Alhaji had a television set which he would bring outside onto the veranda. It was large like a crate and people would come from across the area to stand and watch it. Alhaji himself would choose the station, the visitors would eat chicken pieces, share malt drink and talk loudly over every programme. It was usually football, international games or the English Premiership, but sometimes it would be the news or a film. James Bond was Justice's favourite.

'How does a watch open a car?' he would ask. 'How does a pen fire a bullet? Bond is a very clever man. Very strong.'

When Justice was fourteen, Bakia appeared outside the hut one Friday morning with a proposition. It was July and

Justice was on holiday from school. The time was supposed to be spent as his uncle's apprentice.

'Come with me for the day,' said Bakia. 'Your uncle can run things by himself.' The engine sounded smooth like it was running on honey. 'There's football involved. We need a goalkeeper.'

Bakia was about five years older than Justice, his hair cropped closely at the sides and razored into a flat oval on the crown. He was broadly-built, leaning toward chubby, and had recently taken up a daily regime of jogging and press-ups which had filled out his top half, whilst having little impact on the rest. He dressed in 'London-wear', shirts with buttons and long sleeves which he'd seen the students wear in Accra, and hip-hop training shoes of which he seemed to have several pairs. Bakia spoke on a level with grown-ups and to Justice he had the brightest future of anyone he'd ever met.

They headed eastwards out of Effiakuma for a change, until the traffic thinned, and the cacti and waist-high grass tumbled onto the edges of the road. Then they took a sandy path which led to a village where the huts were built into a hillside so steep it was as if they were stacked on a shelf. There were dwarf goats and dusty chickens, and children squatting, pants down, on the sides of the road. The most well-kept and lucrative business appeared to be that of the coffin-maker who displayed his wares like sports cars in a showroom; polished black caskets lined with crumpled white silk, cream painted, layered with varnish, delicately carved, hung with golden handles. If they lived so wretchedly on this side, they weren't prepared to tolerate it on the next.

The residents had placed a plank across a deep sewage gully, which flexed under the weight of the bike. The air began to lighten and Justice felt a breeze blowing from the direction they were heading.

On one side of the coast road were boulders piled high against the waves, on the other was a row of British colonial buildings, Georgian in style, with the dates of construction carved ornately above the doors. Weeds grew from cracks in the stone pillars, the shutters had been painted pink and green, and washing hung from every glassless window.

They passed over a narrow bridge where an inlet fed water into a sandy bay and Bakia pulled off the road. Justice remained on the back of the bike.

'He won't know you've been here. I won't tell him. No one will. You don't believe what he told you, do you?'

'I am not happy here,' said Justice. He was studying the line of polythene bags, plastic bottles and lost fishing nets deposited by the high tide.

'All medicine men say they have four eyes. It's meant to scare you.'

A group of boys had appeared over the far side, kicking a ball between themselves.

'If he had extra eyes to see the spirit world,' continued Bakia, 'then how come you can hide in our house for days on end? The spirits would be telling him where you were, wouldn't they? They'd be jumping on his head and pointing at my bedroom window.'

'You should have told me we were coming here.'

'Listen, the sand is soft. Good for goalkeeping,' and Bakia ran to join the others.

On the journey home, the bike's single light barely made a dent in the darkness. Justice tucked in behind Bakia, his shorts cold against his legs from the sea. He would have stayed at Alhaji's but for the fact his Koran and homework were at his uncle's and tomorrow, Saturday, he would need them first thing at the Madrassa, the Islamic school, where he'd studied since he was five.

When he arrived home, there was a single candle burning. 'Where have you been?' his uncle was sitting on the edge of the bed, the red sash which he wore for his rituals still hanging loosely around his waist.

'Can I get in, I need to rest.' Issah and Zuleyha were asleep, and there was little room to stand without treading on a stray limb.

'I heard Bakia's bike.'

His shorts were nearly dry now, so he wouldn't change them.

'I heard Bakia's bike,' his uncle repeated, more loudly.

If he was up early enough he would go via the snuff shop. It felt like he had a cold coming on.

His uncle grabbed his wrist, pulled him sharply to the edge of the bed, and held Justice's forearm in front of his mouth like a joint of meat. Then, starting from the elbow, he began to lick. Occasionally he paused to moisten his tongue. 'Salt!' He spat on the floor.

Then it began. Uncle Ibrahim threw Justice's arm to one side, spun him around, and locked his head in the crook of his elbow. Justice could smell the fire. There were knuckles rubbing his scalp. They were both sweating. He tried to slip his head through the hole. It tightened. More

15

knuckles. He lashed out his arms behind him. They couldn't reach. His uncle seemed to have the strength of many. A hand was trying to locate his ear. It moved over his face, trying to find its bearings. Then it rubbed. Like it was trying to clean out a stain.

'Sand. Look at the sand,' Ibrahim was still talking. Then, without releasing his head, 'You were not born here. You are a stranger. The sea doesn't know you. The sea can take you.'

He twisted Justice off balance so that he fell to the floor. Then he beat him. When it was over Justice ran out into the warm night. The door of the Madrassa was open and so that's where he slept, beneath the desks on the concrete floor.

Justice attended lessons there every weekend and never once played truant. He worked hard, learning Arabic and studying the Koran. He found the words exhilarating, and would say them aloud, learning passages and prayers by heart. He was excited by the similarities he found with the Old Testament and wanted to share the discovery with his friends. Justice Amin was fourteen and wanted to be a preacher.

His inspiration was his Islamic teacher Ibraham Musah. He was a tall, gentle man, in his late twenties, with a face round like the moon, and a smile so regularly exercised that the muscles had knotted his features into a permanently benevolent beam. He wore a flowing Islamic shirt, the chest pocket clipped with pens and stained with ink blots and which reached down to his leather, open-toed sandals.

Musah toured the local villages on a cream-coloured scooter, preaching Islam and helping out with any life event that might require religious guidance. Wherever he went, an entourage would follow, chattering and laughing as he moved from house to house, cradling babies that were thrust into his arms or performing ablutions on the bodies of the dead. It was part of his role to register the newly born and recently deceased of Effiakuma, which he did on scraps of paper, always intending to transfer his notes to the official record. But they bulged from his wallet or fell from his pockets along with the bottle tops, telephone numbers and pieces of chalk, and no one minded at all.

Sometimes Musah would be swept along from one grateful family to the next so that his bike was stranded several miles away. Whenever that happened he knew that it would be waiting for him outside the mosque again, spirited back by whoever found it.

Along with his other duties, Musah was in charge of the Madrassa. It was situated about fifty strides from Justice's home, a long, low, sand-coloured building consisting of three small classrooms with uneven stone floors and peach-coloured walls bruised by dirty hands. The rooms were arranged side by side and only semi-partitioned, allowing Musah to keep three classes on the go at the same time. One patch of wall was painted dark as treacle. It was the school's blackboard where Musah wrote his flowing Arabic script for the pupils to copy. The shuttered windows had vertical metal bars like those of a prison but to Justice there was nowhere in Effiakuma he felt more free.

'My world is getting smaller,' he told Musah one day. 'It's becoming tighter, so that the only place I can breathe is in here and at the mosque.'

Musah had arrived at 5.30 a.m. to find Justice sleeping

beneath the desks again. Beside him was the Koran and a Bible which he'd brought from school.

'The idol fills our house,' Justice said. 'There is nowhere to escape. Even if I close the door so I can no longer see its face, the spirits are always thick around me. I cannot pray in the house without it interfering.' The call to prayer was just beginning from the speakers at the mosque next door.

'Your uncle will not change what he worships,' said Musah. 'Don't think about him. Try to clean him from your mind and if you do that you will be free even though he is always around you.'

'One of us will have to die for me to be free,' said Justice. 'When I think of him, I think I want to be out of life. If it is an illness or an accident I do not care. I just need to breathe.'

'You can still turn your life into anything you want. Do not let your uncle distract you. Remember how I taught you about Shadrach, Meshach and Abednego in the Old Testament?'

The pair sat in the half light as Musah recounted the story. 'The three men were ordered by their king to worship a golden idol. When they refused, he had his soldiers tie them up and hurl them into a fiery furnace. But, to his astonishment, it was the soldiers who burned, not the three men. They could be seen walking calmly around in the flames, accompanied by a fourth figure who was an angel. When they left the fire, they were unharmed and the ruler abandoned his idol and told his people to worship their God instead.'

Musah rose to his feet. It was still dark outside, but he could hear the men removing their shoes at the entrance to the mosque. He gestured for Justice to follow and the two of them went together and prayed.

That year, the Reverend Grant Methodist School came close to expelling Justice. His uncle had repeatedly failed to pay the fees and then, of course, there was the matter of his irregular attendance. In the end, though, they recognised the problems he had at home and allowed him to stay. Anyway, they liked the boy. It was why Mr Ashie had come into teaching, to tame pupils like Justice.

He continued at school until the summer of 2003, when he was fifteen, and then he left. Even though he stayed on at the Madrassa it meant that, during the week at least, he had no excuse to be anywhere other than at home.

'You must take over the business,' Uncle Ibrahim said to him one day. 'That is why I taught you.'

'I will find other work,' replied Justice. 'Don't bother me.'

The medicinal side Justice was comfortable with; boiling roots, wrapping leaves in tight pads so they could be pressed onto wounds, grinding seeds and bark. It was The Head he wanted nothing to do with.

'We have a different god. Your idol is full of evil. I will not worship it.'

'He has watched over you since you were a child. Without him we would have nothing.'

'We do have nothing,' replied Justice.

'Foolish boy! You will worship the idol. I instruct you to worship him.'

Justice flew into a fury. 'Allaah is Most Great, Allaah is Most Great, Allaah is Most Great.'

His uncle shouted over him, 'You will worship the idol so that you can look after me when I am in old age.'

'I take refuge with Allaah from the devil, from his pride, his poetry and his madness.'

'Oh, yes! Ask him for a sign. Prove to me that he is there. You cannot! My god is with us all the time.'

'You do not know what is right or what is wrong,' screamed Justice. 'Only God knows. I will not do as you ask. You are not my father!'

The arguments were frequent. Sometimes Justice would disappear for days at a time, staying at friends' houses or sleeping outside. He relied on charity for food; Bakia's father would buy him fish or meat, others would give him bread if they spotted him wandering around town. He couldn't remember the last time his uncle fed him.

Always, though, he'd return. The hut still contained the dying embers of familiarity and he couldn't leave Issah and Zuleyha alone. There would be little conversation with his uncle, but he'd help prepare potions, and speak politely to the customers.

On one of the last occasions, he sat outside by the fire whilst his uncle prepared himself in the back room. The customer seemed uneasy. He was just inside the porch, on the waiting bench, shifting and fidgeting. On the ground, beneath a piece of wire gauze, sat a brown chicken. Justice heard the drum and the bells begin.

It was evening and car lights flashed by, silhouetting the hawkers, and the men on their way to the washrooms.

Inside the porch, the candles were placed on pieces of board, one in each corner and a cluster around The Head. He always used red ones.

Today his uncle wasn't going to treat a stomach complaint or poisoned blood. He was going to treat his client's fear. The door of the bedroom swung back and out into the porch strode his uncle. Without acknowledging the man on the bench, he headed straight for the chicken. Around his ankles were silver balls the size of marbles which rang as he moved. His wrists were adorned with bracelets of black and white stones, and around his middle was wrapped his bright red sash. Tucked beneath one arm was an ageing dondo drum, stretched with cream goat skin, which he beat rhythmically with a stick. In his hand was a horse's tail, the stump bandaged to a leather handle, which he waved frantically around as if writing urgent messages in the sky.

'Tuuna,' Ibrahim whispered, then more loudly, 'Tuuna!' and he stroked the tail over the wire gauze. The idol sat impassively in the corner. There was a pause in the drumming whilst his uncle lowered himself awkwardly into a squat. The customer still hadn't spoken. Then the chicken was in the air, swinging by its throat. 'Tuuna. Take. Tuuna. Take.' It made such a fuss some of the candles were blown out.

Justice was outside tending the cauldron. He preferred to keep a distance during the ceremony itself. Instead he stirred the leaves and watched the traffic pass by. At this time in the evening it was mainly buses returning workers home. The customer was just inside the door, body rigid, face mesmerised.

His uncle pressed the crest and squeezed the head so small it seemed like it belonged to a snake. Then, with the other hand, he grabbed a wing, and threw the body into a spin. The chicken turned several times, so that its neck was pleated like a rope. The idol didn't have long to wait now. The head came away with a sharp tug. He held the bird by its feet and let the blood drain onto the black encrusted head. It collected in the eyes and the mouth, spots fell to the ground and dripped from the wall, and his uncle's hands were bathed in it. He started shouting, sounds, animal sounds, screwing up his face, gabbling and grimacing and searching for something.

'Tuuna, Tuuna.' The sounds came again and Uncle Ibrahim spoke like he was fluent in them. Then he drew a breath, shut his eyes, and there was quiet.

A hunting knife lay on the floor by the bench. Beside it was a saucer of black powder. His uncle was listening. Listening to what Tuuna was telling him. Then he turned and told the customer to remove his shirt. The man's body was thin. Ibrahim took the blade, turned the man's arm to face him, and made a small incision about an inch long across his bicep. Then he took a pinch of black powder and packed it into the wound. He did the same in the crook of the elbow, and again on the forearm, three cuts on each arm.

'The medicine will work,' Uncle Ibrahim said to his customer. 'Whenever you encounter danger, shout and the spirits will be with you. The danger will go away.'

In the final months, his uncle's dependence on the idol seemed to deepen and Justice withdrew further. Shortly after leaving school he found work on a building site.

'A European building site,' he told friends proudly, 'blocks of flats. Neat and tidy.' It was a carrying job: buckets of cement, stone blocks, metal rods the length of goalposts, all in swirls of dust from the fearsome machines brought in from the city.

One evening on his way home from the site, he saw a crowd gathered outside Bakia's place. They were standing on the veranda, maybe five deep, some balancing on chairs for a better view. Justice was unaware of any televised football. He crossed the road and saw on the screen a line of grimacing men wearing only shorts and displaying their muscles to a cheering crowd. There were flags draped behind them, and photographers leaping around the stage. It was 'Man Ghana 2004', a body-building competition live from the Presbyterian Hall in Accra.

At work the next day, Justice filled a bucket with concrete and rocks, and stood a metal rod in the mixture, upright like a tree. When it had set, he hit the bucket and it slid away leaving a heavy stone lollipop. He was like James Bond, he told himself, constructing something to help him escape. Then he did the same with the other end, and when that had set too there were matching bulbs of solid concrete. Justice now had his very own dumb-bell and managed to transport it all the way home on the bus. When he arrived, he stored it in the porch in the opposite corner from The Head.

Weightlifting became part of his regime. He rose at 4.30 a.m. to walk to the mosque for prayers, returned home to the dumb-bell and left for work at 6.30 a.m. At the construction site, he found himself a quiet place for Dhuhr Prayer,

Asr Prayer and Maghreb Prayer, and then returned home at 7 p.m. In the evening, he lifted weights again before Isha'a Prayer and bed.

His construction job was over in a couple of months. 'My spirit is not in tune with their spirit,' he told Bakia. 'When I try to pray, they say, "No, it's time for work." If I pray before lunch they say, "Why do you leave work early?" If I pray after lunch they say, "Why are you back so late?" Their work gets in the way of my prayers.'

They were pushing weights together, counting who could do the most. 'You know, even the bike shop is not good,' said Bakia. 'The others, they laugh like they are happy, but how can they be happy? Everything is so tight. Even if someone says "There is no money today," they will still go there. They will stand outside its locked door and be happy just to smell the oil.'

It was Justice's turn. He swung the dumb-bell into position across his shoulders and began.

'Even in Accra, the money is small,' continued Bakia. 'Maybe some building work, or some sewing, but it's small. Enough to pay for the next day's bus ticket, not enough to move on. If I want some peace, if I have a wife, even, one day, children, where do I go? Look at me. I live with Alhaji, like a baby.'

Alhaji had once been a wealthy man. He'd owned a fleet of trucks which transported cement north to the rainforest city of Kumasi. To show his gratitude for his good fortune, he'd built a mosque near to his unfinished house in Effiakuma. It was a low sturdy building, made from cement, with a sloping tin roof. There'd been some excitement about its opening, but one day a digger came along and flattened it to make way for a new road. And so Alhaji promised to build another. The next one was made from wood, a smaller affair, which was thrown up fast, and collapsed even faster. For the third attempt, Alhaji returned to cement, and began construction right next to his own home. It was to have two rooms, a brick minaret, and running water for ablutions. But he went out of business and the mosque remained half finished. It was soon inhabited by goats and chickens.

'He keeps thinking one of us will go and bring back money,' said Bakia. 'He sees I am strong. He is confused why I am still here.'

In the summer of 2004, Abu Bakia began retreating from his life in Effiakuma. Justice would search for him at the motorcycle repair shop or ask the girls at Madam Molly's. In the courtyard with its tunnels and crumbling arches, Alhaji would shake his head and say he hadn't seen his son for days. When they did meet he had little time for football or bikes and would disappear again in a hurry without telling Justice his plans.

'Momentous things are taking place,' he would say, but that was all.

The rainy season arrived and Justice created projects to keep himself indoors and out of the way of his uncle. He asked Musah if he could paint Arabic phrases on the walls of the mosque. It was a plain windowless room, with a low ceiling of polystyrene tiles and rickety three-armed fans. On the concrete floor were goat skins for kneeling and in one corner a length of orange rope attached to a plastic bucket which was used to draw water from the well for ablutions. The only feature on the wall was a blackboard upon which was written 'Zaawiya Mosque Committee' and which listed the amounts of money donated from the community.

Justice sat with his Arabic dictionary at his side, carefully copying the outline of each phrase onto brown paper. Then he traced them onto the wall with a pencil and filled the letters with carefully applied black paint. One of them read, 'Every rich Muslim should go to the Haj.'

On other days he would sit alone in the Madrassa, rain rattling down on the metal roof, an English version of the Old Testament on one side, a Koran in Arabic on the other, translating, cross-referencing, exploring. 'There is only one God,' he would say to Musah. 'There are just different paths to the same destination.'

It was when the skies cleared and the sun scorched the dry earth again that Abu Bakia vanished. Justice met Alhaji on the road one day. 'He's moved on,' he said. 'I think to Libya. After that, maybe to Europe.' And Alhaji looked pleased.

Justice's world was tightening further. He had no work and the fights with his uncle were growing more violent. He began searching for calm among the elders of Effiakuma.

Directly across the main road from his uncle's hut, down a passageway beside the hardware shop, was an area of open ground. It was covered with coffee-coloured dust and ringed by the open sewer. At the centre of it, beneath a single impressive palm tree, was Attaya Base. It consisted of nothing more than a square cement platform, buffed by years of bare feet and covered by a corrugated metal canopy.

There were no walls, the roof was suspended by wooden posts, and the place looked little more than a shelter from the sun.

There was a single step up to the platform, beneath which the men deposited their shoes and then congregated in a corner, around the tea-maker. He boiled and re-boiled the tea, stirred in mountains of sugar, poured it from a great height into a small pot, boiled it again so that it frothed yellow, and then, when he was happy it was rid of its bitterness, he poured it into shot glasses which were passed around on a silver tray. It was green tea, but when it was prepared this way, it was called Attaya.

The men then sat back and discussed the issues of the day, dressed in long Islamic shirts and kufi hats, glass in one hand, prayer beads in the other.

They would say, 'Justice, can you fetch us more tea?' and he would obey.

They were the wise and the thoughtful. It would be disrespectful to refuse. He would rush off to the store and buy them supplies: tea, banku, charcoal, water, and in return they would give him food. They also allowed him to join their debates.

Bush's re-election, the war on terror, the Tsunami, the elections in Iraq, the Koran, the Hadith, the Sunnah, whether the Ghanaian midfielder Michael Essien would move to Chelsea for more than twenty million pounds. They would stop debating only when it was time to pray.

Sometimes Musah would arrive on his cream-coloured scooter bringing the latest news from families across town. 'Bakia's father is waiting for money. None has come through yet,' he reported one day. 'But now the boy is in Libya it will start, Inshallah.'

A glass of tea was hurried over to Musah, who sipped it noisily and placed it back on the metal tray.

'Three others went from here in the same week. Some families have not yet heard whether their boys are in life or in death.'

One of the men threw his arms in the air and whispered a prayer.

'Travelling the desert can take many weeks. God has already been with them. He has seen that they are willing to make sacrifice. They must sacrifice to succeed. Even at the point of death they must still sacrifice so that others can survive. It is a lesson I have taught them. And if they reach their goal then it will be God who has allowed them to do so, and God who has brought good things to their families, and their families will thank God five times over every day.'

'And will he go further? Will he go to Europe?' someone asked.

Musah beamed and signalled he wanted more tea. 'If God is willing,' he said slurping noisily. 'Then yes, Bakia will go to Europe.' Then he left.

In late summer 2005, when Justice was seventeen, his uncle entered the house one day and prodded him.

'You must leave,' he said. 'If you cannot pray to it, then you must go.' He prodded Justice some more. 'Why are you still here?'

'Stop bothering me. This is my home,' said Justice turning his back. 'I will leave when I am ready.'

'You close your ears to the truth. Tuuna has offered you

his secrets but you have refused. There is nothing here for you now.'

Justice turned and shouted, 'Tuuna will take you to Hell.'

His uncle rushed over to him and slapped him across the head and face, 'You insult my god. You will suffer. Out! Get out!'

Justice was still on the floor, reaching out his arm to block the punches, 'I take refuge in Allaah!'

He tried to grab his uncle's hand, and was surprised by his strength. Then the hunting knife appeared. In a moment it caught against his forearm and a slender red thread appeared.

'Out now, I will have nothing more of you,' Uncle Ibrahim was still shouting, but the punches had stopped.

Justice supported his arm beneath his elbow and the two watched as the thread broadened and began to drip. He went into the porch for some leaves. There was quiet for the rest of the day, but that evening Justice left. Three days later, when the house was empty, he returned and took money from his uncle's hiding place beneath the bed. It was enough to take him to Accra and perhaps beyond.

Chapter Two

Justice spent his first month in Accra lugging crates of pineapples and fish, and in return the market traders gave him food. It was a hectic place. Young men carried cardboard sheets laid with glass jewellery, tin bangles, and watches which said, 'Rolex' or 'Gucci'. Others sold T-shirts from bamboo rails, 'American Rapper', 'Rasta Man!' There were football shirts too, some were white and bore the union flag with 'England', 'David Beckham' or 'Wayne Rooney' written across their fronts.

Justice would eat banku from a tin plate, and watch the girls glide serenely by. On their heads they balanced stacks of eggs, suitcases, bowls brimming with fresh water, even sewing machines and once a small fridge. There was one corner where the sacks of grain were kept. It was shaded and dry, and there were wooden carts propped against the wall. It was where the men gathered to do business.

'You want Libya?' they whispered. 'We show you safe route. Very little money.'

They wore leather shoes and London-wear shirts, and always seemed busy, organising groups of twenty or more. In Accra, anyone planning to cross the Sahara began their journey at the market. Justice would sweep by carrying his boxes. 'Hey, when I want to go, I will tell you!' he would say, and they would wink and point, and continue talking quietly into their phones.

At night, the market boys made fires and cooked rice. Sometimes, there would be leftover chicken livers or discarded fish and they'd go in the pot too. A few wanted to be taxi drivers or electricians, but most were saving to escape.

'Across the desert,' they would say. 'Maybe to Libya. They have money there. The wages are good. Even the poor have cars.'

All of them knew someone who had made the journey. 'My brother, he is wealthy now. So much money. He sent it home. The work is easy. Just lifting in the market made him rich.'

'What about Europe?' Justice would say. 'Europe is my target.'

'Ah Europe! If I am able to. If God allows. There is no better place.'

Then they would climb into the wooden fruit carts with the tractor-sized wheels and sleep.

One day, when Justice was waiting for work, a man called Nuru approached him.

'Why aren't you in school?' he said. Justice explained that he was seventeen and had finished his studies.

'What did you learn?' asked Nuru.

'I learned the Koran,' replied Justice. 'And how to draw.'

'Ah, you draw?' Justice followed Nuru to his embroidery shop, where he sketched trees and leaves and roots. Nuru was impressed and hired him straight away. Later he taught him how to use the machines. The shop was narrow but deep. There were two levels. Justice sat at the back on a platform. There was barely enough space for him to sit among the rolls of material. Beneath him, on the lower level, close to the door, two tailors sewed cotton jalbabs which they separated into two piles on the floor. There were the plain ones, which were ironed, folded and packaged, then there were the ones which required embroidery. They were passed upstairs to Justice. Although it was traditional Islamic dress, Christians would order too. He sometimes designed garments with ornate crosses which clients would wear to church.

Six coloured bobbins spun on top of the loom, releasing threads into a system of vibrating hoops and needles. Justice fed the material through, manoeuvring it so that the colours fell around the neckline and the sleeves of the jalbabs. His favourite pattern was the one with golden interlocking stars. There was a bench on the lower level of the shop where Nuru measured out lengths of cloth. It was white plastic, covered in pen marks and scribbled numbers. At night, it was where Justice laid out the fold-away mattress he had bought in the market.

The shop was a gathering place. Young men would lean in its doorway, smoking and drinking coffee, or play chequers on the upturned crates outside. One of the regulars was Eddie. He shook everyone by the hand and draped an arm around their shoulders when he spoke. He always said he was far too busy to be loitering at Nuru's place.

'When I returned home I had enough money to buy a taxi,' he told Justice one day. A year in Libya, that was all. 'If I go back, I will make enough to buy two.'

Justice was leafing through the book of designs. 'It is Europe I want,' he said, resetting the machine.

'My friend, it is Libya first and then Europe. You cannot do one without the other. If you do not go to Libya, there is no Europe.'

The bobbins began to rattle and rotate, and Justice prepared the material.

'For Libya, I can help,' Eddie continued. 'The route is dangerous. We must plan it before you leave. Even then there are risks, but they are smaller,' he was sitting close to Justice, his chair pulled alongside him in the cramped space. 'I will phone people. They will take you in a car or truck. They know where the police wait. But I need your money now. They only work when I am paid.'

Nuru was cutting cloth on the white bench. 'These are conversations fit only for the market,' he bustled, and then waved Eddie out of the shop, following him onto the street to make sure he'd gone. Eddie shook Nuru warmly by the hand before he left.

Over the months Justice was approached by several others, both at the embroidery shop and in the market-place. People mentioned names of roads, contacts in bus stations, towns and villages that were unfamiliar and sounded far away. 'Don't trust the others,' each one warned. 'Best price is with me. Low price, low risk.'

'Let me think,' Justice would reply, and then when they'd gone, he would write down everything he'd heard in a notebook.

One evening, Eddie appeared in the shop looking agitated. 'A group is leaving next week. It is a good time to travel. There are places available.' He indicated for Justice to clear his mattress, and the two drew chairs around the white cutting table, where Eddie sketched the route. 'The money, I need it soon. These men want many in the group, not just two or three. It is not worth their risk for small numbers.'

'How much?' asked Justice.

'I could do it for 300 dollars. That is the best price. Anyone who asks less is lying.'

'Let me think,' said Justice.

'When you arrive, the money will be good. You can sew clothes all day. Make Muslim dress in Libya and they will pay you well.'

'Let me think,' said Justice. 'I need to pray.'

The alleyway was in darkness when Eddie and Justice left the shop. People were poking around in the debris from the market, there were fires burning and children cooking corn on wooden sticks. At one kiosk, the owner had fallen asleep, arms folded over his counter, whilst the chicken spat and burned on the grill. Justice and Eddie walked together to the main road, and shook hands.

'I will see you next week for the money,' said Eddie. 'God bless.'

Justice said nothing. He set off back, past a billboard for the new 6 series BMW and into Nuru's shop.

The next morning, by the time Nuru arrived, Justice was ready to leave. 'I have found new work,' he said. 'Back in Effiakuma.'

Nuru fetched two glasses and brewed him some tea. 'Justice,' he said, 'the desert is hard. More than a thousand miles across. Even when you are young and fit, it can take your life. The guides will try to trick you. They collect your money and then leave you, and when you are alone, every direction looks the same.'

Justice tried to fish out a tea leaf with his finger.

'There are bandits too. All across the border. Before you reach Libya there are Bozo fighters with guns.'

Justice had given up on the tea leaf and was smiling nervously at the floor.

'Why don't you return to your family?' Nuru suggested. 'You are more help for them in Ghana than you are dead in the desert.'

'Let me think,' said Justice, and headed off to the bus station.

At the State Transport Company depot he consulted his notebook. 'Kumasi' he read, then joined the others in the queue.

The road out of Accra was slow. At every set of lights, hawkers reached through the windows offering lotto cards and plastic bags of water. Once they were north of the city, the traffic cleared – it was mainly buses and lorries, settling in for the five-hour drive.

By evening, the villages were laid out neatly in green fields, woven grass huts against a backdrop of banana trees. Everything seemed clean and fresh. Behind the plantations

Justice could see the towering canopy of the rainforest – cocoa trees, teak and silk-cotton. It was gentle here, things felt less tight.

As they approached Kumasi the air turned pink with road dust, the streets narrowed and the traffic thickened. Vendors were crammed along the roadside, selling ornate hardwood furniture and silverware. One man displayed hundreds of turtle shells which he'd converted into bowls and ashtrays. Justice saw white people, picking through the stalls. Most were his age, with heavy-looking bags strapped to their backs. There were none in Effiakuma, nor around Nuru's shop, and he wondered how it would feel to speak with them.

The depot was seething. All the buses in central Ghana seemed to have arrived at the same time. Horns blasted, drivers shouted and any crack in the traffic was immediately filled with a micro-bus, luggage teetering on the roof, faces squashed against the windows. When they finally swung into a bay, Justice jumped down and headed for the smell of food. He chose chicken feet, yellow and crunchy, and treated himself to a bottle of malt drink.

'You want Togo? Cape Coast? Côte D'Ivoire?' Everyone seemed to own a vehicle. There were men rounding up passengers, carrying luggage, clearing paths through the traffic, and all to the deafening soundtrack of a thousand competing radios.

Justice had written 'Bawku' as his next destination and made his way to the waiting point. There was already a queue even though the bus didn't leave until morning. He found a spot against a concrete wall and sat quietly alongside a youth eating dates from a paper bag.

'Babs,' the youth said. 'I am Babs.' Babs was from a village called Bakado, on the Cape Coast, near Effiakuma. He was taller than Justice, with a shaved head and a voice unsuited to his body. It came out deep and ripe, like that of a fat man, and his laugh was silent, just a rhythmic nodding of the head where the sound should be.

'How far are you going?' asked Justice.

'Maybe the desert,' said Babs. 'I told my parents I will cross it but I will wait, wait until I see how big it is.'

'And if it is too big?'

Babs chewed for a while, then slipped the stone onto his palm and dropped it onto a pile with the rest. 'It's not easy. My parents, they collected money from everyone in the village so that I could travel. "Even small, small work will pay," they said. Now they are waiting. Everyone is waiting. The money I send home will be shared by many.' Babs offered Justice a date and Justice took one.

The journey to Bawku seemed endless. Other boys had arrived in the middle of the night and were now dotted around the bus, plastic bags on their knees, all heading for the same place. Rainforest gave way to savannah and Babs disappeared up the bus. He returned with news that one of the others had been to Libya before.

'No problem,' he grinned. 'The man says we have an invitation. Gaddafi has invited us in. He welcomes everyone from Ghana.'

Justice turned in his seat and saw a figure with sunglasses and a leather sports bag. 'The man is lying,' he told Babs. 'He's never been there. If Gaddafi welcomes us in, why does he put police in the desert?'

They stopped at a filling station. It stood by itself on a sandy plain. To one side was a tower made of metal rods. It rose higher than a tree and at the top was a giant metal tank.

'Water!' shouted the driver, and they clambered down to find children selling flat bread and a woman mixing stew by the road.

'Rat,' said one of the passengers. 'It's okay when it's boiled.'

In the afternoon Justice tried to sleep but the sun hit hard against the window. There were fewer villages now and they seemed empty; no one on the sandy paths, just an occasional goat dozing in the shade. The huts were round and windowless, made from thick orange mud which had dried hard in the heat. The desert was starting to take hold but there were two more countries yet before they reached the Sahara.

When they arrived in the town of Bawku it was dark and the air was thick with burning wood. The drive had taken thirteen hours and now they were poised less than ten miles from Ghana's northern border. The depot was a patch of orange dust with a hut and a concrete shelter. It was silent, lit only by the beams from the bus headlights. Broad sandy paths led away into town, but they were deserted except for donkeys and goats silhouetted against abandoned fires.

'If you have friends to visit here you must wait until morning,' said the driver as they climbed down. 'No one is allowed to walk the streets when the sun is gone.'

A child appeared beside Justice. 'Sleep?' he said and offered a rolled-up mat from beneath his arm. Justice gave him a coin and took one.

The driver began unloading bags from a flap on the side of the bus. 'The people here, you won't see them coming,' he said. 'They can make themselves invisible and fly with the wind.' He had their attention now. A dozen of them crowded around, eager to hear more.

'You are in the Dagbon region. Four years ago, they had a festival of fire to thank the spirits for their magical powers. The King was here, the King of Dagbon. So were his enemies. They began to fight. Some fought with the King. They cut his head from his body. Then they put his head on a spear and danced. The King's men and his enemies still fight. Everyone here fights. That is why the streets are empty,' the bus driver turned and walked towards the unlit hut.

There were dozens already asleep, women and children wrapped beneath colourful cotton, their men watching the sacks of grain or peanuts resting beside them. Justice, Babs and the others laid their mats on the floor. Justice had a plastic jar of Shitor, a tomato paste cooked with shrimps, and chilli. He'd brought it from Accra, black and sticky, along with a plastic spoon. 'You can keep it for a month,' he said. 'And it won't spoil.' He ate a half measure and offered the same to Babs.

'Like hot dates,' said Babs, arranging his belongings into a pillow.

The next morning they left Bawku in a minibus, bound for the Ghana border. When they arrived they saw a solitary figure, sitting beside a pile of rubble, behind a large office desk which was battered and scratched, a missing leg replaced with bricks. The man was an immigration officer. He sat proudly at the roadside among the disorder, dressed in a turquoise military-style shirt with a braid draped around one shoulder. When the bus approached, he stood in the centre of the road and waved them to a halt. Everyone was ordered to step down.

'You have passport?'

'No,' replied Justice. 'I am coming to Burkina Faso, that's all. No further.'

'Paperwork of any kind?'

'No. I thought you were friends with Ghana.'

'Mmm. Open your bag.' Justice put it on the table, and invited the official to look inside. The Koran, a T-shirt, 'What's this? Shitor? Are you heading for Libya?'

'No!' said Justice. 'I can't go that far. Just Burkina Faso.'

'But Shitor, it will last for many weeks. You have pickle here too. This is travellers' food. Desert food. If you only visit Burkina, there is no need to have it. Tell the truth. Are you going to Libya?'

Justice shook his head and hunted for an explanation. The immigration officer was wicked, it would cost him nothing to let him through. Babs was already at the other side, queuing to get back on the bus. 'I hate your food,' said Justice. 'The food in Burkina. I can't eat it. I am here for a month, so I bring Ghana food with me. That is all. I am not going to Libya. I am staying in Burkina. No further.'

The officer looked at his face but Justice was concentrating on the floor. 'It is illegal to go to Libya without papers,' the officer opened a thick book of receipts and began writing. 'If they catch you they will put you in a prison under the ground.' He thumped a purple ink symbol onto the receipt and put his hand out for the money.

On the road north to Ouagadougou, streams of orange dust rose magically into the sky. Sometimes they slid across the road, twisting and gathering, before collapsing in a cloud. Traders sat beneath tatty beach umbrellas, selling water from petrol cans. Camels passed by, their owners wrapped white against the morning sun. The driver threw open the door for ventilation and Justice leaned his face into the breeze. Babs did the same.

'Boys must have left from your village before,' Justice said. 'Why is everyone waiting for you?'

There was a lorry up ahead, carrying wood through a swirl of dust. It almost filled the road.

'Many boys have left before,' said Babs. He pulled his shirt over his nose and closed his eyes until the lorry passed. 'Last year five went. They left together. Even my parents gave them money. One was the cleverest boy in my school. When he left, his teacher came to say goodbye and told him if there was enough money in Libya, he should bring some home for the village, and the rest he should keep for his education, so that he could go to college.' They both pulled up their T-shirts for the next overtake. 'But the boy never phoned. None of them did. Nobody heard from any of them again.'

The tarmac was patched and puckered and the sand drifted across it in shallow waves. Traffic was slow. When a vehicle broke down, passengers would stand in the middle of the road whilst it was levered onto rocks for a wheel change. Torn tyres and broken axles lay half buried in the sand. Abandoned cars had been picked clean – seats were the first to go, then fan belts and spark plugs.

The bus slowed for a sharp bend and two police officers stepped out. They signalled for it to pull over, and ordered everyone to the side of the road. Justice took his receipt from his pocket and waited in line.

'The language, what is this?' whispered Babs.

Justice shrugged. There was a lengthy conversation with the driver. A man on a bike stopped to watch from the other side of the road. More appeared. Women removed the huge silver bowls from their heads and waited. There was some jostling. Everyone wanted to translate. Finally the driver extracted himself.

'Anyone with passports, back on the bus,' he said. 'The rest, you need to wait.'

A couple of middle-aged men left the line and climbed back onto the bus.

The two officers then broke up the crowd, which re-located a few paces away on a pile of rocks. The police seemed satisfied, and turned their attention back to the line.

'They need to take you into town for paperwork,' said the driver. 'They say the chief is not here today. You must go with them into town, so that he can sign the papers tomorrow. They want me to drive you there.' The officers were waving the men off the rocks now, ordering them back onto their bikes. 'Or, you can pay a small fine now, and that will be it,' said the driver. 'We can move on.' He collected the money.

Justice counted five further road blocks on the way to

Ougadougou: police, customs, immigration, forestry commission, then police again. The Burkina capital was obscured by a haze of pink dust. It settled in Justice's hair and stuck to the sweat on his temples and the bridge of his nose. The stall holders on Charles De Gaulle Avenue had wrapped their heads like nomads as they cooked stew in giant silver pans. Motorbikes weaved among the traffic, carrying sacks of cola nuts or live chickens, twenty at a time, hanging by their feet from the mudguards and handlebars. The huts were brick. Some had been converted into shops by erecting four wooden stakes at the front, and balancing a sheet of corrugated metal across them. They had names like 'Boutique Prix Bas', 'Le Salon', and 'Madame Monique's Boulangerie'.

At the bus depot, the vehicles were a collection of salvaged body parts: Frankenstein buses, so overloaded their doors had to be tied together with rope. Justice stepped across women selling French sticks and pain aux raisins from plastic sheets, and entered the main building. It had a dark cement interior with a single ticket window and a wooden door. Beyond it he discovered a prayer room. On the floor was a large cotton mat, embroidered with pictures of minarets and domes. He knelt and rested his forehead on the cool material. The din from outside barely penetrated here. His earlier prayers had been mechanical, snatched during water stops, but now he could concentrate. He began reciting the words slowly in his head. Then the door swung open.

'Hey, we need to hurry,' Babs had entered. 'There's a state bus heading for Niger. Everyone's boarding. If we miss it, there'll be no more till tomorrow.' Justice didn't move. His forehead remained on the mat. 'I am praying,' he said, without looking up. He tried to refocus. Babs closed the door quietly, and left him.

When Justice stepped outside into the Ougadougou haze, the temperature was in the mid-thirties, but locals wore jackets and woollen hats against the wind. Babs was in a crush of travellers pressed against the closed door of a state bus. The driver sat inside filling in paperwork.

'A state bus is more money,' Babs said when Justice squeezed in beside him. 'But if we take a private one, they will stop us at every checkpoint and make us pay. They say the state ones are waved right through.'

The seats filled quickly. Men joined the route from Côte D'Ivoire and Togo in the south, Mali in the west. They swept across Burkina in their thousands, a migration of the young and ambitious, all heading for the same place: Niger, the desert state. From there the Sahara stretches northwards, over the granite mountains of the Aïr Massif, across hundreds of miles of barren wilderness and on into Libya.

Their plan worked – they weren't stopped once on Trans-African Highway number 5, until they arrived at the Niger border late that evening. An immigration officer emerged from behind a grass fence. His office was a clay hut above which a flagpole rose twice as high as any tree and leaned precariously in the wind.

Another officer joined him. 'Passports' were lined up on one side of the road, 'no passports' on the other. Justice stood beside Babs towards the rear of the queue.

'Où allez-vous?' the officer said to the first boy.

He frowned and looked at his feet. 'Est-que vous allez en Libye?' There was no response. The officer backed away and began to address the whole group. They stared back at him, blankly.

Justice had been speaking Fante with Babs. Only those from Burkina Faso, Côte D'Ivoire and Mali spoke French, not the Ghanaians. He put his hand in the air. 'I am from Niger,' he said. 'I am returning home to see my family. This man is my friend.' He said the words in Hausa and they understood.

It was the language used among the Muslim communities of the Cape Coast and Justice had spoken it with his uncle and with Musah at the Madrassa. It was also one of the official languages of Niger.

'Okay,' said the officer, leading Justice along the line. 'Ask this man where he is going.'

Justice turned to the Ghanaian at the front of the queue and, speaking to him in Fante, said, 'He wants to know where you are going. Don't say Libya. If you say Libya he will know you have lots of money in your pockets for the journey and he will take it from you.' Then he turned back to the officer and said in Hausa. 'He says he is staying with friends in Niger.'

The guards were pleased they had an interpreter and rewarded Justice by allowing him to pass through the border without payment.

The bus travelled on through the night, crossing the Kennedy Bridge over the Niger River and stopping to unload in the capital Niamey, before heading out on the fourteen-hour journey northwards towards the desert city of Agadez.

When Justice awoke, the landscape was burnt brown, the earth and sand scattered with boulders and small bumps from which thin yellow grass was trying to grow. The huts were like upturned bowls, smooth and rounded, and made from thick clay which had baked and cracked in the sun. When they stopped for water, the villagers had slaughtered a goat and were grilling each limb with the fur still on. The head was cooked too. On the side were goat intestines wrapped in stomachs, fleshy sacks of offal to take away. They were cooked on charcoal with powdered spice and a squirt of something yellow. Justice chose a spoonful of Shitor from his bag instead.

In the afternoon, the sand became smooth and rippled like the sea, and there in the distance the city of Agadez appeared, adrift in the desert. There was no wood or brick, no tin roofs. The place looked like it was carved from sand. Windowless cube houses, broad empty roads, even the minaret of the Grand Mosque was made from Saharan clay.

More migrants joined the flow. They came from Benin, Nigeria and Cameroon in the south, Chad to the east, Congo and the Central African Republic. Their numbers were swelling. They sat on street corners and collected around the bus station or the district from where the huge desert trucks departed north. Among them were university graduates, skilled professionals, mothers with children, families fleeing conflict and persecution. Up to seventy thousand migrants pass through Agadez each year, two hundred every day, all in transit between sub-Saharan Africa and the Mediterranean coast.

'Not from here,' said Justice. 'Everyone leaves from here.

It's where the police expect us to start. They know these routes.' He showed Babs his notebook. 'Arlit,' he said. 'The bus continues through to Arlit. It is north of here, high up in the Sahara. There will be cars and desert trucks. We should cross the desert from Arlit.'

The bus disgorged passengers into the depot, where the people smugglers were waiting. 'Quickest route to Libya . . .' they whispered. 'Cheapest route . . . Safest route.' Justice and Babs remained beside the bus, the rest melted away in taxis and down side streets. The passengers queuing for Arlit were mainly old men, carrying provisions for their families in remote districts. Justice wouldn't let the bus out of his sight, in case it left without them.

On the road to Arlit the desert became golden waves, and in the east the black granite of the Aïr Mountains sent ripples through the sky so it seemed they were on fire. The bus stopped and let an elderly man step down. He was wrapped in white cotton with a turban half covering his face.

'Is this Arlit?' shouted Justice.

'No,' the others smiled. 'You have many stops yet,' and the bus pulled away into the unchanging landscape. Justice asked the same question every time they stopped.

When they were close, the bus passed by an isolated canyon where mechanical diggers were biting chunks from the cliffs. 'Uranium,' someone said, and Justice saw the hole went down so far there was a pool of green water gathering on its floor. Other machines were ploughing piles of rubbish and mixing them with sand. Goats and a group of women waited patiently by to see what was unearthed.

The bus finally pulled into Arlit when the warmth had drained from the evening sky. The depot was a tin hut, in which several migrants had already bedded down for the night.

'We need turbans,' said Justice. 'Turbans against the sand.'

They approached a group of Tuareg tribesmen seated around a brazier, their camels hung with plastic water bottles, sacks of dates, and strips of brightly coloured cotton. Justice and Babs stocked up.

'Like Bozo fighters,' said Justice, and Babs nodded rhythmically as they stood in their T-shirts and jeans, heads wrapped so tightly only their eyes were visible.

Later Justice laid his cotton on the ground and prayed. The buses went no further than Arlit, from now on they'd be relying on people smugglers to move them across the desert.

Chapter Three

'Libya, Libya ... Safe route ... No police ...' The people smugglers were up early, their vehicles congregated around a busy patch of sand, from where tyre marks charged off in all directions across the open desert. There were military-style jeeps, 4x4 pick-ups, and livestock lorries with caged compartments. The largest group, though, were the desert trucks. They had wheels as tall as a man and carried bulging grey sacks of nuts, leather and cotton piled five times higher than the truck itself. The sacks hung from its sides and from the driver's cabin, dangling from ropes, with water bottles, petrol cans, even bed frames, until the truck itself vanished and was replaced by a shaggy grey beast. The migrants clambered up makeshift ladders to perch high on its back.

'JD' was beneath the bonnet of a pick-up truck which was already half full. He wore a black desert turban which was so long it covered his shoulders and tumbled half way down his back. His eyes were hidden by oversize sunglasses and he had a moustache which looked as coarse as hog hair and drooped past the corners of his mouth down to his chin.

'He will have done it many times,' reasoned Justice. 'He is old.'

'Three hundred dollars,' said JD, wiping the oil from his hands. 'There are a hundred ways into Libya. I know them all.'

'Which route will you take?' asked Justice.

'The police are patrolling the eastern routes, so we will go west for a while, close to the Algerian border, and then move north, around the Massif de Tarazit. I have friends on the other side. They tell me when there is change. It will take maybe two days, that is all.'

Justice and Babs agreed. JD took their money and groped around beneath his voluminous gown to find a pocket.

They didn't leave until every space on board the pick-up was filled. Justice sat on top of plastic petrol cans, his feet dangling over the side, others stood against one another, or clambered on top of the driver's cabin. There were twenty of them in that small space: Ghanaians, Nigerians, others from Togo and Chad. Some wore thick coats with woollen hats and sunglasses, others heavy sweaters and desert turbans.

They cut two fine lines across the barren plain, spitting fine sand into the air. Another pick-up pulled in behind, migrants packed on the back, and they drove in formation for most of the day. Justice pulled a fold of his turban down over his eyes. All he could hear was the muffled monotone of the engine and the fluttering of cotton against the wind.

His tongue stuck to the roof of his mouth and when he put his teeth together there was grit.

Darkness fell at seven o'clock and there was not a light to be seen. JD continued for a while, headlamps off, and then pulled away from the track and into a valley. In the driver's cabin was firewood tied with string and a plastic bag containing a teapot and glasses. JD made camp by the side of the truck and the migrants wandered off into the dark to find boulders to sit on.

'You are going to stay in Libya, or continue to Europe?' he asked when they were all seated.

'I have a brother who lives in London,' said one. 'He sends pictures of his house. In his room there is only him and his wife and their child. I will stay with him.'

JD balanced the metal teapot in the flames.

'Sweden is good,' said another. 'They like blacks in Sweden. There is work there.'

Babs was eating dates. 'In Spain too, they have work,' he said. 'Construction and carrying and they pick oranges from the trees. The weather is like Africa. Sweden is too cold.'

JD wrapped his hand in a rag and began pouring tea.

'England is best,' said a Ghanaian. '. . . No need to learn a new language. There are many blacks there, many places to stay.'

And they chatted for a while, transported to cafés in Rome, Madrid and London, as they sipped green tea in the chill desert air.

Late on the second day JD stopped on a plain with black peaks visible through the haze to the east. He came round the back of the pick-up and made an announcement. 'We have just crossed the Libyan border,' he said. 'You are safe now.'

They whooped and clapped, and some of them jumped down to feel the new land beneath their feet.

The first settlement they came to was a village of domed clay huts. There was a small market selling nuts and dates, and a group of tribesmen resting their camels around the edge of a well. Other than that there was nothing. It was a barren, hopeless place.

'There is a problem with the engine,' shouted JD. 'You have to get out. I will find a place to fix it.'

Whilst the others looked for shade, Justice and Babs wandered over to the well.

'It is empty,' said a tribesman. 'We have to climb down and dig. Then there is water.'

Justice peered into the blackness. It smelt stale, like sewage. 'Which way is Tripoli?' he asked.

'Tripoli?' replied the man. 'Tripoli is a long way. You are still in Niger, this is not Libya.'

Justice and Babs raced back to the road. Some of the others were ahead of them. 'He has gone,' they said. 'He has left us.' And they never saw JD again.

That night they built a fire and slept in the open. Justice's Shitor was running out and they were low on water. There were no cars in the village, only camels and donkeys. Their only hope was that a desert truck might pass through, looking for provisions.

The crowd at the well were intrigued by the newcomers. 'You are thin, you fit down the hole very nicely,' they said to Babs. To one side of the hole was a rusting car wheel around which a length of rope was coiled. The other end was attached to a bucket which hung over the lip. 'We are strong, we can hold you.'

'How deep?' asked Babs.

'Not deep. We will give you dates when you fill the bucket.'

Babs pursed his lips.

'When you are down there, you can refill the bucket many times and the whole village will be grateful.'

They tied the rope around his waist, and Babs sat on the edge, the bucket on his knee. Inside was a teacup. 'You will need that when you reach the bottom,' said one of the tribesmen. Then Babs swung round, two men took the strain and he disappeared beneath the earth.

'It will be more difficult to get him back up,' said Justice.

Even though the hole was small, beneath the surface it opened into a cave, so that Babs was away from the sides, dropping gently through the dark. The sweat on his back and forehead grew cold, and the rope dug into his skin. Three silhouettes hung above him in the circle, and when he shouted, his low voice filled the space, clattering around him like he was in a crowd. Eventually his feet came to rest on a large flat stone. It felt smooth and dry and when he pulled it away, more stones lay beneath. It was some minutes before he'd cleared enough to feel the sand. It was cold and heavy, and as he burrowed with his fingers it began to slide down the sides. Deeper, and there was water, a pool of it, up to his knuckles. The hole was the right size to fit a teacup. Each time he scooped, it was replenished in seconds. It took nearly half an hour to fill the bucket twice and then Babs signalled he'd had enough.

It became part of the routine. Several times a week they would visit the well, Babs would be lowered inside, and whatever water he managed to bring to the surface he would barter in exchange for food. Justice survived by collecting firewood for a baker, who paid him in bread. The man was some sort of desert nomad, his features Arab, his skin drawn tight across his cheekbones, toughened and freckled black by the sun. The villagers liked the man, and when business was good he even let Justice help knead the dough and bake it in a clay oven.

He and Babs still had a small amount of money left, which they'd intended for the final leg of the journey, across Libya to the coast. Now they would need it to buy a place on the next vehicle out of town. It was four weeks before one arrived, a giant shaggy beast of a truck, like the ones they'd seen in Arlit, and there were several migrants already on board.

'The Libyan crossing is dangerous,' said the driver. 'The police have equipment which they put against their eyes so they can see for many miles. We are heading for Algeria, to a small oasis close to the border. I will take you there but no further. I know a guide who will take you the rest of the way. You will meet him soon. Pay me now, and him later.'

Justice and Babs handed over fifty dollars each, and clambered up to join the rest. As they waited, a man appeared from behind a hut and shook hands with the driver. The two chatted for a while and Justice realised it was the nomadic baker. He looked different now. A large desert turban was wrapped grandly around his head, and his gown was indigo cotton, drawn tightly into his waist by a wide leather belt from which hung a dagger. When they'd finished talking, he climbed up the side of the truck and sat beside Justice.

'My home is far from here,' he said. 'This man takes me part of the way whenever he passes through. Anyone who wants to go further, they come with me, across the mountains. It takes five days on foot, maybe more, and then we arrive on the Libyan border.'

As the truck pulled away, he began collecting money from the others. Justice and Babs were last. When the baker turned to them, he seemed transformed. His eyes shone indigo like the colour of his gown, and his expression was no longer one of boredom but of calm intensity, wise, almost regal.

'How much?' asked Justice.

'You were good to me,' said the baker. 'When I needed firewood, you searched hard. From early in the morning, you always kept the oven hot. Now I must repay you. Whatever money you have, keep it. You will need it when you reach the other side.'

Two days later, they were walking out of a sleepy oasis town in south-east Algeria with thirty others, towards the craggy plateau of the Tassili N'Ajjer, led by the nomadic baker, now their guide.

'You must stay close,' he said. 'If you become lost in the mountains you will not find your way out alive.'

The terrain began with isolated mounds of bronze rock, but as they progressed, the mounds rose higher and over-lapped, until they were towering stacks of sandstone, through which the path weaved higher and slimmer. By the end of the first day it had become a system of channels with sheer sides and cool floors. At each turn they found tributaries, leading away from the main path, some of them blocked by falling rocks, others ending in vast lakes of sand.

'Tassilli N'Ajjer means plateau of the rivers,' said the guide. 'Now the water is all gone and only the sand flows through.'

During the hottest part of the day they rested. Each time, the guide would slip away and return with armfuls of sand-grass and dried Saharan Cypress. They cooked tinned tomatoes and rice, and then brewed tea. Many of them were carrying dates, but Justice was the only one with Shitor. When the sun cooled, they walked again, sometimes well into the night.

On the third day, progress was slow. They were climbing a gully which had collapsed at each side, sending a slew of rocks and scree about half a mile down the mountainside. It was so loose in places, the stones slipped beneath their feet and cascaded towards the men behind. The sun shone directly overhead and whichever route they chose was without shadow. About halfway along, the guide turned left along a passageway and they emerged into a sand basin with high stone walls. To one side was a solitary man sitting on a boulder. He was dressed like them: jeans, training shoes and zip-up jacket, but his desert turban had fallen to one side. There was no sign of his colleagues.

'Hey, brother, are you lost?' shouted one of Justice's group. The man didn't respond.

'He needs no help,' said the guide. 'Leave him.'

As they walked on, Justice saw that his jacket had fallen open and there was paperwork protruding from an inside pocket. He left the group to inspect. The man's head was resting on one shoulder, so that half his face was out of the sun. The other half, the exposed side, was black like melted plastic. There was a water bottle wrapped in sackcloth by his side. Justice lifted it and it was empty. He reached out for the papers, hoping they might be travel documents. They came away easily, yellow paper folded into a stiff square. He held them for a moment and then changed his mind, slipping them back into the man's pocket and muttering an apology beneath his breath.

The corpse was the first of many. Others they found resting in caves, or lying face down on sandy plains. Some were partially covered by sand, just their jackets or turbans flapping in the wind.

Justice started out with two litres of water and rationed himself carefully. By the sixth day he was swilling it around his mouth and trying to conserve it by spitting it back into the bottle, but the impulse to drink was too strong. His saliva had become so thick that even a date took several minutes to chew and swallow. After he'd finished, his tongue would stick to the roof of his mouth. He tried to breathe only through his nose but his nostrils became hot and sore, and the dust still irritated his throat.

'How far?' he asked.

'Don't talk,' replied the guide. 'Talking wastes energy. It allows the sun into your mouth. Keep your lips tight and you will make it.'

They passed tall stone arches and rocks like giant mushrooms, and when they looked back they saw the place they had come from – a distant orange plain beneath a blanket of haze. On the seventh day, they stopped mid-morning to rest and Justice went behind a rock to urinate. Halfway through he stopped, thought for a moment and then released the liquid slowly into his cupped hand. It was dark yellow and although it was strong in salt, it moistened his mouth and relieved the back of his throat. He passed the rest into an empty water bottle.

'You have urine?' asked Babs, when he told him. 'I have none. My belly is on fire and when I try to release, there is nothing there.'

'Does anyone have water they will share?' asked Justice.

'No, everyone is close to dry. Maybe I should take some of your urine.'

'It will not be good for you,' said Justice. 'Only the owner should drink it.'

Babs went to ask the others and returned smiling, 'I took some of his urine. It was fine. Just enough to help me swallow.'

On the seventh day, when they were nearing the peak, they came upon a small camp hidden behind rocks. The shelters were made from animal skins stretched across wooden frames. There were camels and burning fires and men drinking tea. The migrants walked slowly towards them and when they reached the edge of the fire, some fell to their knees and wept.

'These are my friends,' said the guide. 'You are close now.' And that night they drank water and ate ginger pickle and slept well.

They remained in the camp throughout the following day and then, when evening came, their guide walked them a short distance to a high ledge. 'The border,' he said.

'Behind you is Algeria, in front Libya. Go now. The lights you see are a town called Ghat. It is two days from here. The police are watching. Walk only at night, and hide during the day.' He shook hands with Justice and then the migrants began edging down the slope, stretching into a line which lengthened and eventually broke. Justice and Babs were in the lead group. The journey down was less arduous. At some points the route became so steep, they half ran, half skated across the scree, faces pink with sand-dust and sweat. Early on the second morning they reached the bottom.

The plain was grey and lifeless, more like grit than sand, with small stones which formed spiral patterns as if they had been shaped by the wind. In the crease where the mountain met the floor was a jumble of rocks which had fallen and collected in heaps. The group kept among them, uncertain when to break cover. Ghat was still a mile away but they could see its band of shivering palms.

They crossed a gully and on the other side, found three abandoned clay huts. 'We could stay here until dark . . .' said Justice, '. . . rest inside, before we head for town.' They had cool sand floors and black stains where fires had burned.

'Maybe walk further, see if there is a place to cross,' said Babs.

They noticed tyre tracks, which stopped beside one of the huts, and then disappeared off behind the rocks. At the other side of a grit bank was the start of a path. There was desert scrub pushing between the stones and the route dipped onto the floor of a shallow valley. Then they heard barking.

'We should turn around,' said Justice.

'No,' another replied. 'The villagers will treat us well. They will know the safest route to town.'

As they spoke three masked men appeared, with dogs straining on ropes. They wore dark military-style clothes, and their hoods had holes only for eyes, not mouths. Each of them cradled a gun. One put his hand in the air and gestured for the group to approach.

'Papers?' he said in Arabic. 'Do you have papers?'

'If I had papers,' said Justice, 'then I wouldn't be crossing the desert. I would be in a plane.'

The man's eyes swivelled in his mask. Then he moved along the line. 'We have been watching you for two days,' he said, pointing to a pair of binoculars. 'When you were right up in the mountains we saw you. There are many police here, every day we see blacks on the mountains.' Then he returned to Justice. 'Now you are in trouble,' he said, and pointed a gun at his chest. 'Walk. Walk to the truck!' There were five of them in the group. Justice wasn't sure what had happened to the rest.

For three weeks he was detained in a police cell at a town called Bargat. There were twenty-five of them crammed into one room, all of them migrants. They slept on the concrete floor and ate porridge made from dried bread and water. One day the guards entered and picked out several men. 'You,' they said to Justice. 'We are taking you to a different place.' He rose and left. Babs tried to follow.

'No, only him,' said the guard. 'You stay here.'

Outside, a tall truck was waiting. The guards pulled back a metal door and shouted for people to press further inside.

Justice clambered on board and the door was shut behind him. 'Don't push . . . stand against the side . . . there are women on the floor.'

The engine started and the truck lurched into gear. Justice was in a metal box, squeezed tightly into the back corner. The face of the man beside him was so close that, when the truck took a corner, Justice felt his bristles rub against his ear. The only ventilation came from a slit high in the metal wall. It was also the only source of light. Justice was soon bathed in sweat and wiped his face on someone's shoulder jammed beneath his chin. Occasionally they would stop to pick up more migrants and the cool air would rush in before the door slammed and the engine started up again.

The truck reached its destination late that evening. A metal side-door swung open, and those closest to it began to disembark. 'Jump, jump!' a voice shouted. There were cries of 'No,' and 'Please leave her,' and Justice could see arms reaching inside to drag the migrants out. As they fell forward they covered their heads with their hands. 'Jump, jump,' the voice continued, and Justice was pushed forwards in the crush.

The first blow caught him across the shoulders. There was another on the back of his thighs. He was looking at the ground. Sand. Boots. And he was running. There was a metal door in a brick wall. Nothing else.

Around forty Africans were sitting in the half-light of a cell. All had their backs against the wall, apart from one who was lying on the ground, face to the floor. When Justice and the others entered, the men lowered their heads to their knees and remained like that until the guards left. The room was taller than it was long. The high ceiling was made from corrugated metal, the walls were sheer, and near the top were square windows, 'Not big enough for a head,' thought Justice. The new arrivals stood around examining their bruises. One of them had been caught on top of his head.

'How many live here?'

'We don't know,' came the reply. 'There are other rooms. We hear the doors open and close. We hear people but we don't see them.'

The man wore a T-shirt which was yellow as though it had been boiled in tea. His tracksuit bottoms carried rust coloured stains, and his feet were bare.

'How did they catch you?' asked Justice.

'Doing lampa-lampa. Many of us were doing it. We had paid the money. The police, they were waiting for us. Somebody told them. They caught about half of us. Some ran into the desert. Then more cars came and they took us to different places.' He gestured to a man sitting on the other side of the room. 'He was with our group. We were all doing lampa-lampa.'

'Lampa-lampa? What is this?' asked Justice.

'We were on a beach,' replied the man. 'With a boat. We were about to cross the sea to Europe. The rest were caught in the desert.'

'What about him?' Justice pointed at the man lying on the ground.

'They say they caught him stealing. He was in town. It is a small place. They say he was in a shop and the owner saw him take some bread. He's been here longer than anyone. Even when he sleeps they come for him.'

The prison is called Qatrun, and is situated in a barren

landscape of gravel and sand. To the west are the gigantic golden dunes of the Idhan Murzuq; to the south several hundred miles of Sahara before Niger and Chad; to the east nothing until Egypt; and to the north the Libyan interior, scattered villages and towns with about five hundred miles of desert to cross until Tripoli and the coast. Justice was marooned in one of the most isolated prisons on earth. There was nothing here but this. The only sounds were those it created.

Behind the metal door was a square patch of gravel. It was completely enclosed by four brick walls. Three of them had a single door through which there was a cell. The fourth was the one through which they'd entered. There was nothing in the gravel square apart from a concrete tank filled with water. It was long enough to take a lying body. Around it were pieces of equipment, ropes and lengths of wood.

Away from the main block were a number of clay domes, like the ones Justice had seen in Niger.

'The guards' quarters,' said one of the inmates. 'When they enter the cell, don't look at them. You must not catch their eye.'

They came on the first morning, carrying short lengths of hosepipe which had been filled with sand and stones and sealed with fire. One of them held a broken car aerial.

'One Abd, two Abd, three Abd,' they began.

Justice wanted to look up. He knew Abd meant slave.

'Hey Abd! You. Moving.' More of them stepped into the cell. Their boots were black and dusty, with padding around the ankles. They walked past Justice and stopped at the man on the floor. 'You, Nigerian thief.'

He didn't move, but said in Arabic, 'Itaqu Allah.'

Justice was astonished. He discovered later the Nigerian thought it meant 'forgive me'. It didn't.

They set on him. One of them hauled his body upright so that he was sitting against the wall. Another took a step back so that he could get more force. The other prisoners were all shouting now, shouting to stop and the guards were lashing out, hitting whoever came into range. The men were scuttling for cover but there was no cover so they crammed into corners one on top of another, some of them trying to hide behind a sheet in the corner, and there were boots among them and laughter. Justice kept his head low to the ground, his arms folded on top and the blows were like hot metal when they came.

'Itaqu Allah. Itaqu Allah.' When it subsided the Nigerian had gone.

'Itaqu Allah?' said Justice. 'The man should not say it.'

'He always responds like that when they come.'

'It is a warning,' said Justice. 'It means "Fear God!"'

The job of cooking was a privilege. It had been awarded to three inmates from Justice's cell. Some months before, they'd helped build another clay dome for the guards and although they'd originally been promised their freedom, that had later been downgraded.

They cooked outside on a fire: rice, flour, tinned tomatoes, sometimes macaroni. The food was brought into the gravel square and served in plastic bowls. Each cell took it in turns. The men were divided into groups of five, one bowl between them. They ate with their hands. The drinking water came from a tanker parked outside. One of the prisoners was chosen to walk there accompanied by a guard. They would fill four or five plastic containers, or 'gallons', and return with them to the cell. Then, after lunch, that was it, they wouldn't be allowed out again until the following day. Even though there was a concrete tank of water in the gravel square, the prisoners never drank from it. It would be several days before Justice discovered its purpose.

When the Nigerian returned to the cell his eyes were swollen like eggs. He said nothing and slumped back onto his mat. There was blood on the top of his head and his feet were cut on the soles.

The men were never told how long they would have to stay, or what it would take to get them out. Sometimes the cooks would return saying, 'The guards need money. If you have a 100 Dinah they say you can go free.' Some of the prisoners had even paid twice.

Fridays were best. It was holy day. The guards began drinking on the Thursday night and by Friday morning they needed a lie-in. They might even stay in their domes until after lunch. The prisoners could relax. There were no beatings on a Friday. Sometimes the guards would choose five or six prisoners and take them outside for a game of football. On one such occasion, two of them escaped. They had no plan. No idea of how to get to the nearest town. So they wandered around in the desert whilst the guards set off after them in jeeps. There was nothing to hide behind. No houses. No trees. All they could do was lie down in the sand and wait. When they were caught, they were dealt with in the gravel square.

'If they deport you,' said one prisoner. 'They will not

take you home. They will drive you into the desert and leave you. If you are lucky, you might find another vehicle, so you can come straight back in. If you are unlucky, that will be the end.'

One morning when the guards entered the cell, they took Justice. He hadn't even caught their eye. They'd shouted at him and struck him with an aerial but he'd never looked up. It had happened to nearly everyone else and so it was, he reasoned later, probably his turn.

In the gravel square the rope was out. The guards were preparing a thick piece of wood which forked into two at the top. They instructed Justice to run around the perimeter. He jogged slowly, trying to preserve his energy for the next stage. The gravel was sharp on the soles of his feet.

The guards swigged from water bottles and shouted for him to run faster. They leaned the forked wood against a wall, so that it was jammed into the gravel at the bottom, and wouldn't slide. After a time, Justice began to tire and they gestured for him to come over. They still appeared quite languid, rising slowly to their feet and brushing the dust from their trousers. Then it was like someone pulled a switch.

One of them had him in a head lock. Justice didn't resist. That's what the Nigerian did. They had the rope around his wrists, he was on the floor and boots were coming in and he was trying to keep his chin tucked into his chest. He was thinking that face to face, one on one, he could beat these men, any one of them, and he hated the indignity of his screaming.

'*I seek refuge with Allah . . .*' his back was scraping against the gravel, and he was near the forked wood now, his feet, they were onto his feet, holding his ankles, and the rope was around them, the same rope, and when they pulled, his wrists and ankles came closer, until they were drawn together in a single knot. *'I seek refuge from the evil of the night when it comes . . .'* The loose end was thrown over the fork and when they pulled, everything tightened, so that the knot rose slowly into the air, and his hands and feet were pointing upwards. One of the guards pulled again until only the curve of Justice's back was touching the gravel, and again, and he was in the air, meat, swinging, and the blows started coming. Onto his soles, taking it in turns: belt, car aerial, belt. He let his head fall back whilst they concentrated on his feet. *'I seek refuge from the evil of the witches who blow on knots . . .'* His blood was moving up his legs into his feet. He needed to play dead. There's no fun in punishing a lifeless body, but he couldn't stop twisting and jerking. Maybe when the next blow comes, or the next, but he was weeping, weeping so that he couldn't draw breath.

Then they stopped. There was a square of blue sky above him and the ropes had gone. If he tilted his head back he could see the outside wall of his own cell, forward and there was the metal door in the wall. But they hadn't finished.

A guard took Justice by his arms, another by his feet, and they carried him towards the concrete water tank. He let them do it. His feet, he was worried about his feet. He couldn't move his toes. He would try to keep them out. They lifted him to the edge. His face was close to the water and they held him there for a while. Then they rolled him in. And it was like the blows to his feet had begun again.

When they finally moved away, he flopped out onto the gravel. 'Into the cell!' one of them shouted, 'not here, into the cell,' and Justice went back on his knees.

It began with a sandstorm, one day in December 2005, two months after Justice arrived in Qatrun. Amber dust leaked in through the high windows and from beneath the metal door. It hung in the air like they were burning a fire. When they went outside to eat, they hurried back coughing and blinking, and the guards retired quietly to their domed huts. It continued like that for perhaps a week. Then a patrol arrived.

The police had found a young African boy wandering in the desert with his father. They'd been trying to find their way across from Niger but had become separated from the others and marooned in the storm. The boy was almost blind. They tried to give him food but he wouldn't take it and his father said he'd not been to the toilet for thirteen days.

Justice suspected he'd been touched by the spirits. 'They've taken his sight,' he said. 'And turned his stomach into clay.'

The guards were curious, and stood watching as inmates tried to feed him rice. The boy refused.

'I need the Koran from my bag,' said Justice. 'And a pan of water from the kitchen.' He kneeled over the water and began reading from the chapter entitled 'The Jinn', the name of the Arabic genies created from fire.

'It is revealed to me that a band of jinn listened to God's revelations and said, "We have heard a wondrous Koran giving

guidance to the right path . . .'" Justice held the water in front of the boy's face. *'Some men have sought the help of jinn, but they misled them into further error. Like you they thought that God could never resurrect the dead.'* He blew on the water, so that his breath reached the boy's face. *'Those that embrace Islam pursue the right path; but those that do wrong shall become the fuel of Hell.'* Then Justice dipped in his hands, wiped the water across the boy's face, and poured what was left over his head. That afternoon, the boy emptied his bowels for the first time and asked for food.

The guards were intrigued. 'The Sheik,' they said to Justice. 'You are the Sheik.' And after that they gave him a job in the kitchen.

From then on, Justice spent his mornings among the smells of bubbling tomatoes, chopped onions, and whatever herbs he could persuade the guards to bring in from town. Before he served the prisoners, he arranged some of the food neatly onto plates and carried it outside to the clay domes. Then he returned with glasses of sweet green tea. He served the prison administrator, and the guards, and even took it to the living quarters of those who were off-duty, speaking to them in Arabic and inquiring after their families.

They said, 'The Sheik should clean for us too.' So he cooked and tidied their rooms and after a time, rather than having to unlock his cell each morning, they told him he should live with them. They watched him carefully, to make sure he didn't stray too far into the desert but other than that he was free to come and go pretty much as he liked.

Justice wasn't in the prison when they took the Nigerian for the final time. They told him later that the burial had taken place somewhere in the dunes. Then, on a Thursday night in January 2006, he realised he was alone in one of the guard's huts. He rose from his mat and wandered outside into the desert. No one shouted after him. The jeeps which were normally parked alongside the front of the prison had gone. The other huts were dark. He put his head inside one. It was empty. The only lights came from the horizon in the north, flickering white flecks in the direction of Qatrun town. It was as he'd hoped. The guards had gone out drinking.

Justice found a piece of rock and carried it across to the prison. He threw it high over the wall so that it came down into the gravel square with a crunch. The inmates understood the signal. Inside his old cell, they began working on the wall around the toilet. The bricks were made of sand and cement, and the top layer came away quite easily from the sodden area around where they relieved themselves. The week before, Justice had given them a metal spike he'd stolen from a guard's hut, and now they managed to gouge out a hole as large as a fist. They poured water inside and scraped some more. Each time, they had to wait for the water to soak in. They didn't want it to run out when the hole was still too narrow to crawl through but too broad to conceal.

Justice stood at the other side, watching for headlights. When he'd first suggested the plan, some of them had shaken their heads. 'They will beat us until we're dead,' they said. 'They will show us no mercy.'

'Well, don't be there on Thursday night,' he'd told them. 'Tell the guards you want to move to a different cell.' And some of them had done just that.

When fingers first appeared Justice grabbed them to show they were through. Water followed, darkening the wall around the hole and Justice set to work with a stone. It was around midnight when the final chunks broke away and the first man emerged. Soon another appeared, shivering and coughing, and helped to pull others through into the violet night. There was impatient whispering and some wanted to set off at once across the desert before the headlights came. One group thought they should split up so at least some would make it, others preferred to stay together so that none were lost. And prisoners kept on coming, streaked with sand and water, until the hole in the wall had delivered every one of twenty.

Chapter Four

They arrived in Qatrun town shortly after dawn and boarded a bus northwards. There were no police and no questions, just a tarmac strip, shimmering and empty, which carried them for four hours across the dramatic dune sea of the Idhan Murzuq. Their arrival in Sabha that afternoon meant they'd crossed the Sahara Desert.

Sabha was a modern town of stark white buildings, overlooked by an ancient hilltop fort. The streets were busy with Arabs and black Africans. 'Some have paperwork to be here,' said a passenger, 'if you don't, then the police will take you.'

As they disembarked into the depot, a small crowd gathered. 'Togo, Togo,' called one man, 'Ghana, Ghana,' another, and the group quickly split, spirited away down back streets and into waiting cars. Justice was on foot with four others, weaving through the market, where nomads sold goatskin bottles and ornate silver bangles whilst their camels dozed in the shade. The few women he saw were covered from head to toe with long colourful gowns. The group followed their guide beneath crumbling mud arches and along narrow passageways until they came to a clay wall, behind which was a yard and a white-washed house. Inside were three bedrooms, occupied by thirty Ghanaians.

'We call it "the ghetto",' said the guide. 'Find a space, anywhere. It will cost you nothing to stay here for a week. Then I organise a bus to Tripoli. You pay me then.'

It was a well-organised operation. The Ghanaian owned the house, and had lived there for five years with all the correct paperwork. He was in regular contact with other ghettos in the area – one for the Côte D'Ivoire, another for Nigeria. Every country in sub-Saharan Africa seemed to be represented.

'I have five ready to go,' he would say on the phone. 'Togo ghetto has eight. if you can find enough to fill the bus by Tuesday, we are ready to go.'

Justice needed to raise money. He left the ghetto before sunrise each morning, and joined the Africans waiting for work by the side of the road. He built fences and cleaned homes, and after a month had saved enough for the fare to Tripoli. It was a private bus, a battered Japanese model, with a sliding door and water tanks strapped to the roof. The driver was dressed in a white shirt and black trousers, so he looked official. The trick, Justice learned, was to avoid police road blocks by travelling across open desert, and only rejoining the rest of the traffic away from towns and villages.

The driver positioned his passengers in particular order.

There were some from outside the ghetto who had passports and were travelling legally. They were placed at the front. The rest were at the back. Justice understood why when they came across a police jeep parked by the side of the road. An officer waved them down, and climbed up beside the driver.

'Passports and papers!' he shouted.

The whole bus spent several minutes searching through bags and pockets. By the time the front rows had produced theirs, the police assumed the entire group was legal, and allowed them on their way.

They were driven to Misratah, a city on the Mediterranean coast where the driver dropped them at the interchange and wished them luck.

'Clean up here,' he said. 'There are many buses to Tripoli, but when you arrive, the police will be watching. If you are covered in dust, they will know you have crossed the desert.'

There was a modern bathroom with rows of clean basins and soap. The passengers stripped down to their waists and washed. Those who had bags emptied them and put all they could into their pockets.

'Don't carry clothes either,' said one of them. 'If the police see black Africans with bags they will know you have travelled.'

The men began pulling on layer after layer of T-shirts and jumpers. Some even wore two pairs of jeans. Everything else was left on the floor.

Justice arrived in Tripoli in February 2006. From the bus he saw grand hotels with fountains and flowering palms. There were shaded cafés where men lounged with newspapers, smoking and sipping coffee, carpet shops with glass fronts, polished roads with gently humming cars, and from the streetlights hung huge plastic portraits of Colonel Gaddafi.

The bus drew into the busy interchange just outside the walls of the Medina and Justice remained in his seat, examining the crowds for uniforms. Most of the people were Arabs, dressed in flowing cotton gowns with kufis and sandals, but he could see Bedouins too, fresh from the desert, and light-skinned men more formally attired in tailored shirts and ties. The pavement was a makeshift marketplace, where plastic toys and cheap jewellery had been laid out on mats and women sat beside cardboard boxes selling cheap dates and peanuts.

The other passengers left the bus and melted into the crowd. Justice did the same, following them towards the gates of the Medina. The air was bathed in mint and spices from the market, and there were many black Africans on the street. They were loitering in doorways, huddled beneath trees, always apart from the rest, but apparently attracting no hostility. The passengers from the bus entered the Medina through the main archway and Justice followed.

It was calmer and cooler inside the old walls. Narrow passageways ran off in all directions, down steep stone steps and through ornate archways. The walls were thick as if carved from rock and occasionally there would be open doorways through which Justice could see children watching television and women cooking on blackened stoves.

The sky scrapers and traffic noise receded, until the streets were no longer paved, but dust and rubble, and the ornate stone arches had been replaced by sheets of corrugated metal. The further they walked, the more black Africans he saw, until finally they rounded a corner near the post office and found at least fifty of them talking into phones and chattering in small groups. Justice heard Hausa, English, Igbo, Arabic, Ewe – everyone was shouting, organising themselves according to the country from where they came.

The Ghanaians had a system for welcoming newcomers. It was like walking into an embassy.

'You are from? . . . Your qualifications? . . . Do you have friends here? . . . Are you staying in Libya? . . . Do you plan lampa-lampa?'

Justice was dispatched with the youngest among them, a boy called Saidu, to an outlying area of town. Saidu had a thin face with wiry hair poking from above his top lip like insect legs. He was neatly dressed in a T-shirt and jeans, and seemed to consider every sentence carefully before he spoke. Justice guessed he was a college boy from Accra.

'There's a spare mattress in my room,' he said. 'The boy who used to sleep there vanished in the night. No one has seen him since. He hasn't phoned, I don't think he will return.'

When they emerged through a giant archway into the din of the bustling capital, Justice noticed something he hadn't seen before. Behind the towers of the Corinthia hotel, there was water and a port so busy, the cargo ships were queuing out to sea.

'The Mediterranean,' said Saidu as they boarded a bus and Justice watched it through the window, until the carriageway crossed inland and the sea vanished from view.

He'd made it to the top of Africa; all that separated him

now from his goal was a band of water. This young man, Saidu, would take him to a house where he could rest and eat. Once he had settled, he could start making inquiries about lampa-lampa. Justice still had a little money from working in Sabha, but he knew it wouldn't be enough. He'd need to find work.

From the bus he could see houses stacked high, one on top of another, in towers taller than trees. He could see no bricks, just concrete as smooth as glass . . . fifteen, twenty, twenty-five . . . Justice tried to count the floors. In some places the walls had been cut away and the rooms opened to the sun, with a rail to stop the people falling off. Justice thought of all the thousands of men and women crammed in there and wondered if Abu Bakia was among them.

As the bus headed east, the towers shrunk and gradually turned on their sides, white-washed blocks with neat square windows. After three miles or so, the bus peeled off the carriageway and doubled back on itself beneath an under-pass at Shara Tis'a. In the gloom Justice could see rows of young Africans on either side of the road, perhaps a hundred of them in all, sitting cross-legged or lying in the shade. In front of each was a collection of tools. There were buckets and cloths, spanners and paintbrushes, some had just a single hammer or spade.

'Waiting for work,' Saidu explained.

The houses thinned out and the tarmac became uneven. There were more black Africans now, many in overalls. Justice could see them in the doorways of dimly-lit build-ings. They were carrying metal rods and cans of dark liquid, dragging around lengths of rope and chain. Some had hoses and were using jets of water to poke debris towards the drains. The buildings were bare brick without windows and outside each was a fenced-off area where wooden planks had been hammered to form some kind of makeshift pen.

'This is Gurji,' said Saidu. 'Our room's behind the market. It's quieter there.'

Outside one of the buildings, a group of workers had cornered a goat. Justice watched as they dragged it by its head out of the pen and, using a knife that looked as long as a man's arm, set to work on its throat. When it stopped moving, the man hoisted it into the air, but it was the next stage of the process which Justice had never seen before. One of the men made a light cut down the length of the goat's belly, not so deep as to open it up, just to bead the skin. He made a similar cut around its collar and tugged a flap of skin free. Then in one breathtaking movement, like he was tearing down a curtain, the man pulled away half the animal's skin. It came away in a single sheet and hung around its waist like a grotesque skirt. He then gathered the hem and tugged it down further, working it down over the difficult bit at the top of the legs. Then he turned, and with the roll of skin across his shoulder, rocked against the horizontal body until the skin flopped off above its hooves.

Justice saw there were dozens of similar bodies hanging from buildings along the road, with men busily slicing away at them, levering chunks of meat into wheelbarrows. What struck him was how they left the heads untouched, skin and fur intact, so that it seemed the corpses were all crowned with scruffy woollen hoods.

When they arrived at the market, the stallholders were clearing away trays of apricots, peaches and dates, piling cardboard crates of watermelons and pomegranates into the rear of vans and beaten old cars. The mint was so plump and fresh, its aroma still hung over the site like a spell. Saidu led Justice to an opening half-hidden by plastic crates behind the toilet block. At the other side was a dust path which opened out into a cul-de-sac. Around its perimeter were disused store rooms, oblong boxes of sheet metal around which rubbish had collected in drifts.

'Everyone's at work, so it's quiet now,' Saidu kicked aside a plastic carton as if he were passing a football. 'Nearly everyone here is Ghanaian. Nigerians live on the other side of the market.' He gestured behind the metal rooms. 'The others, they live all across town.'

'Does no one stop us?' Justice asked.

'Sometimes. Gaddafi tells the television there are too many of us and then things hot up. The police come in and take people away. It goes on for a few days but there are so many of us, they soon give up. Things calm down again.'

They walked past a group of four or five Arab youths perched on empty oil drums to one side of the path, smoking and whispering.

'Anyway, they know most of us want to leave. We're just passing through, so how can we be a problem?'

One of the youths threw a pebble which narrowly missed Justice and Saidu and pinged against a metal hut behind them. His friends fell around in exaggerated laughter, shaking hands with the missile thrower, and whistling the imagined sound of the pebble as it flew through the air. Saidu smiled back uneasily and raised a hand, as if saluting the youth's throwing ability. That provoked more frantic laughter and the two young men walked the next few paces in silence until Saidu gestured they'd reached their destination.

It was a door in a narrow terrace of metal huts, each one about the size of a trailer from a freight lorry. The cream paint had weathered to a grubby yellow and there was a patchwork of rust bubbling through along the joins where the structure had been welded together. The door was made of two metal panels and was stained black around the handle where generations of migrants had pushed it open after a day's work. Someone had drilled a hole just above the handle and a matching one at the same level on the adjacent wall, so a chain could be pulled through. The roof was constructed from several pieces of corrugated metal which appeared to have been salvaged from a far larger building. It overshot the edges by such a distance, someone had decided to fold the jutting bits over the edge. In places it almost reached the floor.

On the right of the door was a shelf which ran across the front of the hut. On it were training shoes and a pile of clothes which had dried rigid in the sun. Against it was propped the wire skeleton of a mattress. Above the shelf, on the largest panel of the hut was scrawled in large pencil lettering '2 Pac'. The same was written on one of the panels of the door. It was the name of an American rap artist who'd been killed in a drive-by shooting in Los Angeles. Justice preferred reggae. Above '2 Pac' was a large plastic sticker with a prayer written in Arabic.

Saidu's hut was smaller than the rest, like someone had

chopped it in two. It took some time for Justice's eyes to adapt to the blackness inside. He could see the floor was just large enough for a double mattress and a smaller one which Saidu explained had belonged to his room-mate. It had been taken over by a pile of dirty clothes, a radio cassette player and a large bag of rice with 'Sharka-tu Libiya' written across it in green lettering. Now, the smaller mattress was to be Justice's.

The walls of the room were bare apart from an Islamic calendar. 'The water used to come in,' said Saidu pointing to the ceiling where he'd taped several black plastic sheets. 'I found them in the market, everyone uses them. Now it is good unless the rain is heavy.'

The buzzing in the hut was of various cadence and pitch according to the size and mood of the insects that would be sharing it.

By seven o'clock that evening, the cul-de-sac had undergone a transformation. Doors were thrown wide open, and men were traipsing backwards and forwards, carrying rice, biscuits and plastic bags containing soft shapes which Justice couldn't make out. They wore stained overalls unzipped and rolled to the waist, oversized trousers drawn in with string, undersized trousers fixed by pins, trousers of indiscernible colour, some stiff with juices, or torn and flapping as they went about their business. Some had sewn neat patches over the offending areas and tried to cut the material in straight lines above their ankles. The focal point was the four gas stoves, upon which were set four large pans. Three of them bubbled with rice and the fourth contained multi-coloured plastic bags which twisted and wheeled in the boiling water.

Justice was invited to join one of the groups. They drained the water from the pan, added tomatoes and oil to the rice and then scraped the thin orange paste into a bowl, which was passed around so that each man could help himself to a few mouthfuls. Cans of cola and Fanta followed. It was a day and a half since Justice had eaten, and he didn't want the men to see how eagerly he awaited his turn.

'So, you're a newcomer? You going to work in the market?' asked one of them.

'I don't know, what would you recommend?'

'Most of us here work with goats, but some of the bigger guys, they shift sand. Do you know how to skin a goat?'

Justice chuckled. 'I don't like blood. I think I would prefer digging or something like that.' He kept his eye on the bowl as it made its way around the stove, counting how many spoonfuls the others were taking.

'You like football?' asked one of them.

'I play in the goal, like Schmeichel,' replied Justice.

'No,' shouted another man with mock scorn. 'You like Manchester?'

'I like them very much.' The bowl had passed to the man sitting beside him. 'One day, if I train hard, I think I will play for them,' Justice added with a grin.

'Well, you can't sit here. You're at the wrong stove.'

The bowl arrived with a spoon and Justice hurriedly filled his mouth in case the man was being serious. He pressed out the juices with his tongue and found it had the same texture as Tuo porridge, but was sweeter like someone had added a spoonful of honey.

'Manchester is not good,' continued the man. 'This is the Chelsea stove, we all follow Chelsea here.'

'Essien!' bellowed another man, as if he'd just seen the player score a goal.

The Arab youths, who had until that moment been smoking on the oil barrels, fell silent.

'We should try not to make so much noise,' whispered someone else. 'And ignore him. This is the Manchester stove. He is the one who should move.'

Some of the men drifted off to the mosque to wash, others dragged mattresses from their huts and dozed in the fading light. Saidu left the stove for a moment and returned with a bulging paper bag. 'Bayrush,' he said, and handed them small pieces of crescent-shaped bread which, when Justice broke his apart, contained a blob of chocolate.

'So, you want to stay in Tripoli, or are you heading across the sea?' asked Saidu.

'I haven't decided yet,' said Justice. 'I need to send money to my brother and my sister, if I die crossing the water, there'll be no one to provide for them.'

'If you choose the right connection man, it will be okay,' said another man. 'They will make sure you get the strongest boat. They don't want to lose anyone.'

Justice sucked the chocolate from the other half of his bayrush. 'How much are they charging for the best boats?'

'Like I said, it depends who you go with. This season will be difficult though, the prices will be high because the lists are already full. You have money?'

'No, I have nothing,' said Justice.

'Well, my friend, I think you're looking at about a

thousand dollars, so you'd better not develop a taste for bayrush or you'll be saving till you're ninety.'

That first night Justice couldn't sleep. His mattress was so tired he could have folded it away like a piece of damp card. The metal room had been gathering heat all day and the plastic ceiling, a triumph of design innovation during a storm, now acted as an airtight lid so the room brewed with crotches and meat. The two men lay side by side in their underpants.

'Can't we open the door?' asked Justice.

'Too risky. They'll guess we have money in here. If the door's open they could walk straight in. They see the chain, and they try somewhere else.'

Each time Justice turned over, his mattress sponged up the latest film of sweat. He tried to resist turning again until the beads broke their surface tension and drew mazy lines down the sides of his stomach. His head slipped around on the plastic clothes bag and he eventually abandoned it altogether. When he lay face down, his nose was pushed into the cloth fabric covering the mattress and the stench in his nostrils was so acrid he sandwiched a hand between the two.

After a while he repositioned himself, with his head near Saidu's feet, close to the metal door. The door itself was buckled slightly which meant that, although at points, it was flush with the wall, there were gullies which allowed the air in, or at least would have done had it not been a breathless night.

'The last man gave the place some ventilation. We were so hot in here one night, he went out to the market and returned with a metal rod so he could lever out the bottom of the door. He did the top as well but we had to hammer it back when it rained.'

Justice could smell the cigarette smoke drifting through the gap and hear feet tapping against the empty oil cans. 'You know a man called Abu Bakia?' he said into the darkness.

'Bakia? I know the name. From Ghana?'

Justice raised his head from the mattress, 'Yes, from my town, from Effiakuma. He had a motorbike, we used to go to football together.'

'I hear the name. I think I hear the name. But there are a lot of names.'

'He's strong,' said Justice. 'Big arms. Big tummy. Like he's fat.'

'All the Ghanaians, they work in the market. If he's still here, he will be in the market.'

Activity began early around the tin huts. By 5.30 a.m. there were doors clanging and men pulling on overalls or making their way to the mosque. Justice removed the chain and let in some air. It was cool like milk and he wandered out into it wearing only his pants.

Outside the mosque, the men lined up with towels around their necks. There were four taps at chest height which constantly trickled water into a stone trough. They were intended for ablutions before prayers but each of the men quickly soaped their hair, then beneath their arms, and finally dunked each part of their body beneath the taps to rinse themselves down.

Later, when the huts had emptied, Justice set out to search for Abu Bakia in the market. At its heart was a large dusty square, to one side bordered by low pink residential blocks, to the other, the workshops which employed the migrants. In the square itself, the tradesmen had returned with their fruits, herbs and spices, selling them from the back of cars or stalls assembled from polystyrene trays and sheets of tarpaulin. They were all Arabs, but occasionally Justice saw a black African rush by, pushing a wheelbarrow full of meat or bowed beneath a bag of sand.

He stopped one of the Africans and asked for Bakia. 'Ask over there,' the man responded, pointing to a row of windowless single storey buildings. 'He works with meat.'

Inside, the walls and floors were caked with black. The only light came from a line of small fires and from the blow torches. It was a long narrow room, with high ceilings and a door at either end. The fresh heads were poured on top of the old ones. Each man had his own pile. There was a uniform of sorts. They wore all-in-one blue overalls. Most had cut the sleeves off because of the heat generated by the work and to stop their cuffs soaking up the spilled juices. Some had rubbed sawdust into the material to help absorb the mess. It formed tight little balls around the chest and knees, and added to the rigidity. Their hands and bare arms looked like they'd been dipped in treacle, which had dried in swirls and smears and left oily streaks where they'd tried to wipe away the sweat.

'Abu Bakia?' shouted Justice across the room. There appeared to be movement at the far end, men lowering their blow torches and looking round for the source of the voice.

'Abu Bakia. From Ghana,' he tried again.

A youth struggled past pushing a rusting wheelbarrow. Inside was a pile of brown and black goat heads. They'd been cut off quite cleanly and those that were upturned displayed concentric rings like an axed tree: a cream-coloured outer layer, then black and red, and finally a bull's-eye of white where the vertebrae had been severed. The wheelbarrow negotiated the small step at the threshold and the ears swayed in unison. Some of the men close to the door turned and shouted behind them.

'Bakia! Bakia!'

Justice couldn't see clearly what was happening or what the men were doing with the heads. There was the smell of gas from the blow torches, mixed with human sweat, and the acrid sweetness of green meat. The air was being sucked in through the door at one end and out at the other where Justice was standing. Some of the workers near the door had taken heads from the barrow and sat them upright in front of them on a table, like they were sitting down to eat. From behind them, a worker was moving slowly towards Justice.

'Hey Bakia, you're looking good,' said Justice, patting him on the stomach. 'How come you still find enough food for two?'

They sat, that morning, in the shade of an unfinished brick wall away from the market. 'It's safer,' said Bakia. 'The Arab men, they don't come here.'

Bakia was living about a mile from Justice, still within the Ghanaian sector. It was eight months since he'd arrived, taking a similar route across the Sahara but without a visit to Qatrun. He'd found work early on and stuck with it.

'Have you got the money for the crossing?' Justice asked.

'Maybe I go back to Ghana. A lot of people die.'

'Come on!' said Justice. 'Why do you work in that place if you are not doing lampa-lampa?'

Bakia leaned away from the conversation with a smile and fiddled with the corners of a cement sack. 'The truth is I haven't decided. If I had the money, *if* I had the money I might go. But the lists are long. Maybe there's no room.'

'Who did you speak to?'

'They are not Libyans. They are African men, blacks. "Connection men". They have lists. You pay money, you get on the list. They are on the phone all day, checking who is ready, checking you have the money.'

'They are black men who take you?'

'No, the black men are the connection men, not the organisers. The organisers are at the beach, they never come into town, in case they are caught. The connection men do their work for them in Gurji. They can move among us with no trouble. That's why they use blacks. No one knows who they are, unless they are doing business with them. The big men, the organisers, they are Libyan. They wait at the beach and when the weather is right and the boat is right, they call the connection man, and he calls you. But you can wait. You can wait a long time.'

Then Bakia grinned. 'How is the uncle with the four eyes?' Justice jabbed his toes into an abandoned pile of cement. The two of them reminisced about trips to the football and Ibrahim Musah on his cream-coloured scooter and the debates they'd had at Attaya Base. They didn't talk of Justice's uncle at all.

Finally Bakia raised himself to his feet. 'Listen, I need to go back,' he said, and Justice followed him towards the market and the workshops.

'What about you Justice, you going to do the crossing?'

'Hey, I've just arrived.'

'You got money though, something to start?'

Justice thought for a moment. 'No,' he said. 'I came with nothing.'

Some days later, Justice caught a 6 a.m. bus back towards the city. It was full of Africans at that time in the morning, but he was the only Ghanaian amongst them. Most of the men travelled in pairs and were more neatly dressed than those at the market. On the main road, it was still relatively quiet, but the farming trucks were starting to arrive, disgorging goats into the pens, before heading back to the fields for breakfast.

The bus looped off the Gurji road and onto a carriageway where it pulled over. Most of the passengers, including Justice, disembarked. The underpass at Shara Tis'a had already attracted a crowd. It was built beneath a four-lane carriageway and appeared to be a recent addition to the Tripoli road system, with high cream stone walls rising to meet the underside of the road. At the top, just beneath its ceiling, the builders had constructed a narrow stone ledge which was wide enough to walk along. Justice could see clothes and bedding hanging over the edge, and understood he'd crossed into another zone where life was organised differently.

The early arrivals had already taken position in the front row, tools laid out before them like prize-winning fruit. A second row had filed in obediently behind them, and a third had started forming behind that. It was the third row that the men from the bus joined, but not Justice. Instead he picked his way to the front and stood on the road facing the rest of them.

The traffic, he guessed, would approach from his left, which meant the most sought after position was in that direction too; furthest man to the left, front row. The powdered cement on the road puffed out beneath his flip-flops and was carried behind him on the breeze.

'Brother, I'm Justice,' he spoke in English, smiling re-assuringly and reaching out his hand.

The man was seated on a roughly-cut wooden box with a handle on either side. It was positioned just inside the shadow thrown by the bridge. He wore a western-style dress shirt several sizes too large, which he'd buttoned at the cuffs and all the way to the collar. His trousers were clean and folded neatly around the ankles. Instead of rubber flip-flops, he wore a pair of matching socks and black polished slip-on shoes. His hair sprouted in little grey swirls around his temples.

'I'm from Ghana. You?'

The man looked around for help.

'He Côte D'Ivoire,' someone shouted. 'No English.'

Laid out before him on a piece of cloth was a row of well-oiled screwdrivers with yellow glass handles. They were lined up with equal spacing between each, in ascending order of size, the blades pointed outwards towards the road. Their owner rose from his box and took Justice's hand to shake it.

'What's in the box?' asked Justice.

More men were arriving now, some took a look at the

crowded underpass and moved on, others scaled the wall, hauling themselves onto the ledge to lie down in the shade. Justice moved to the next man and shook his hand just as he had the first. On the ground before him was a single piece of copper tubing with the ends sawn away.

'He plumber,' shouted another voice, and then, leaning forward to indicate other items of interest. 'Brush . . . painter; Hammer . . . bricker.' But they were the exception. Most had no tools at all. 'If nothing . . .' said the man. 'Any work he can do.'

The new arrivals had rejected the idea of starting a fourth row and crossed instead to the less favoured south side of the road where the traffic was thinner. There was laughter and pointing as the first man positioned himself in the new territory. 'Your hair will grow white before anyone stops there . . . They will take you to the desert today, and leave you there.'

The new arrivals sat on the dust with their elbows hooked around their knees, chuckling and shaking their heads. 'It will be a good day,' one shouted back. 'I pray hard this morning and God told me to choose this side of the road. It will be good.'

'If you had spent less time praying you might be on this side,' came the reply amid more laughter.

Justice continued his way down the front line, like a jaunty general inspecting a ragtag parade. 'Anyone from Ga-na?' He often said Ga-na like that, snapping out each exaggerated syllable like he'd caught a fly in his throat. He was playing the crowd and enjoying it.

He was directed to a short square figure, separate from the

rest, leaning against the wall of the underpass with a finger in one ear and a phone in the other. The man wore a light blue baseball cap with 'Dubai' written across the front, a pair of dark blue Nike bottoms (not bad for fakes, thought Justice), and a white linen T-shirt. The man's name was Victor. He'd already given up on finding work for the day and was just killing time. Here was as good a place as anywhere.

A car slowed and its driver pointed a finger at the man from Côte D'Ivoire. He leapt to his feet, carefully sausaged his screwdrivers in a roll beneath his arm and turned to reach into the box.

'When I first came, I used to sit here every day,' said Victor. 'A man stopped his car like that and shouted that he wanted someone to dig, anyone. About twenty of us ran over. He drove off and then stopped a little further down the road. We ran to catch him up. He drove off again, then stopped. Each time we got to his truck, the same thing happened, he drove off.'

The screwdriver man took a squat metal jar from inside the box. It had a long thin spout, like an anteater, and a trigger which allowed him to dab oil on his tools. Then he turned and climbed alongside the driver.

'Anyway, several of the men became exhausted. They gave up and returned to the underpass, but a few of us carried on, the youngest mainly. We ran, must have been half a mile, the truck stopping and starting. I was carrying a spade. The sun was up and the dust, it was bad, so I stopped and walked back. The next day I heard the driver carried on like that until there was only one man left running. Then he stopped and said, "You're the winner," and he let the man in.'

Another van pulled over and a group of men with hammers huddled round. The queuing system had already broken down.

'Anyway,' said Victor. 'The two men sat in the front of the car. There was no water, nothing, and the brother, he was breathing heavily. They drove and drove until the road was in the desert. The car went further, maybe an hour from Tripoli, maybe two. They came to a big house, and the brother, he was told to dig. He dug in the sand all day and then he went to the Arab man and said he was finished.'

The breeze through the tunnel faltered, then returned with a surge. The two men shielded their eyes from the dust.

'The brother put his hand out for money,' continued Victor. 'And the Arab, he just laughed and walked away. He left him in the desert.'

Justice watched another group crowding round a car. 'Did he go to the authorities?'

'No, how can he complain? They just take him to police station for being illegal. No one can complain.'

Justice returned to the underpass every morning for a fortnight and on two occasions even made it to the front row, but the waiting, the helplessness, it wasn't for him. Most of the others weren't here for the crossing at all. They'd seen Libya on the television. The wages were higher. They'd said to their families, 'Just a couple of months and I will be back.' Then they'd landed at the underpass and fallen into the routine: sending money home, sleeping on the ledge, praying for work. Just one more month. Until they were drifting in a country where they didn't officially exist, sending money to a family which was moving on without them. In the end, they were just a ten digit number at the office of the Western Union in Accra or Freetown or Ouagadougou; the code their wives would need to collect the money.

Victor had a wife and two children in Ghana, the youngest a girl aged four. When he felt her wriggle inside her mother's belly, they'd laughed with delight. But the following day, he'd packed a change of clothes and headed north, stowing away on a desert truck. He'd hidden amongst the cotton shirts and the cakes of salt, on a pile so high it had been tethered to the trailer like a hot air balloon. When he'd left, she'd waved him off with tears, but they'd both agreed it was, 'best for the child'.

Almost every dinar he earned, Victor sent home. It was the thought of his daughter, growing plump and healthy, that shook him awake in the morning and powered his muscles to lift the spade. He kept meaning to return when the time was right but then he became preoccupied with dark thoughts. If he left the underpass he would be depriving his family of all they had come to rely on, all that was good in their lives. The moment he crossed the threshold and held his daughter for the first time, was the moment he failed her. Better she was fatherless with shoes, than shoeless with a regretful father.

'Many men sailed last night.' Justice was cooking rice and tomato stew for some of the men in the tin huts when Saidu arrived with the news. 'Many men,' he said again, hurrying inside and dragging out a mattress.

'There are people missing from every workshop in Gurji. Two from the butchering block. More from the market.'

Whenever there was talk of departures, Justice found himself drawing a deep, involuntary breath, like at Qatrun when he heard the keys in the metal door.

'The pick-up trucks were coming and going all night. They were lucky not to get caught.'

News of departures normally filtered through by sunrise. Empty mattresses, missing food, maybe a note, it was the first anyone knew. Those about to sail would tell no one of the plans, and there was good reason. Of course the connection men knew, they had to, and the people smugglers themselves. Then there was Razak.

'How many?' asked Justice.

'Razak says four boats, maybe five. The weather was good last night. No wind. If God wills they should make it.'

Another group of men wandered down the pathway towards the fires, talking excitedly about the same news.

Justice pretended to be busy with the cooking but was wondering whether Bakia was on one of the boats.

'All separate groups,' Saidu went on. 'They didn't know they'd chosen the same night. Razak says the organisers were arguing on the beach.'

Razak was a tall, athletic Ghanaian with a neatly shaved beard which spelled an 'O' around his mouth. His nose was broad and across its bridge was a crease from squinting in the light, even though most of his days were spent in the dark. His head was shaved, so it was easier to wash away the blood and, like the others, he was rarely seen in anything but overalls. Razak would apologise for himself as soon as he entered a room and just as he was about to leave. He knew no matter how hard he tried, he couldn't rid his body of the sweet, loamy tang of burning flesh.

In the block where he worked it was said Razak even waved the flies to safety, instead of incinerating them in mid-flight. His gentleness was reflected in his voice, a low, soothing whisper, like he was a verbal masseur. Whenever he spoke the men hushed each other quiet so they could catch every word he said. Even the older ones, those in their late twenties, sought out his wisdom. When it came to the crossing, Razak seemed to know more than anyone else in Gurji. It was something of a mystery why he himself still remained. But he never spoke of how long he'd been there, or what was delaying him.

Justice met Razak on his first day at work. The multiple departures the previous night had left vacancies and Saidu persuaded him he could learn the skills he needed on the job.

'You just spit the fire at the head to start. Keep spitting it by pulling this handle.' Razak showed him how to hold the goat's head by its ear and stroke it gently with the flame. The fur shrank into pungent fuzz and fell to the floor. He put the head on a metal table and scraped it down using the blunt edge of the machete. The skin was crisp and came away easily, and beneath it, around the nose and cheeks, were pieces of flesh that he picked off and placed in a small pile. Justice saw that if the goat had white fur, the meat was white too. If it was black, the meat was dark brown like a leg of chicken.

Razak spoke like he was sharing a secret. 'You see, it's very simple work and Master is a good man. He doesn't mind if you take a bit of meat for yourself.'

He slid the head to the edge of the table, pulled open its mouth and pushed the machete up against the v of its jaw, working it into the bone. Then he put his hand beneath the tongue and prised the mouth apart. Justice heard the bone crack and saw that only meat held the jaw together. Razak tapped away with the blade, freeing shards of flesh and poking them into the pile with the rest.

'Justice, can you take the tongue? Just pull it.'

Justice hesitated, then chuckled.

'What is it?'

'You're like a doctor, giving me my first lesson in anatomy.'

Razak nodded thoughtfully and smiled. 'Maybe I should tell my mother that's what I'm doing.' He put the tip of the blade into what was left of the throat, and slit the tongue in half down the middle.

'Now, some people want the jaw but they don't want to see the teeth, so knock them out,' he whispered. Then, he raised the machete to shoulder height and cracked it on the crown of the skull. 'Try not to damage the eyes. Some people want them for their dogs, but they don't like them damaged.' He put his fingers into the wound and pulled, so that the skull snapped into two halves revealing the brain. He cupped it in his hands and placed it separately. There was some oily-looking substance beneath it which he scooped from the base of the skull and dropped into a plastic bag. 'People like this for soup,' he smiled.

Razak had known many newcomers over the years and found they were normally cautious and uncommunicative. They didn't need this time to reflect, it might let in the fear. But Justice was different, smiling and greeting people like he'd been parachuted into a party, not a workshop that could be raided at any moment for illegal immigrants.

The goat's brain was a little larger than a hen's egg but grey and patterned with ripples and creases. Razak took a plastic bag from the workbench and placed the brain inside. On the floor beside him he had a military-style satchel, inside which were tomatoes, onions and a bag of salt. He took out a tomato and an onion, sliced them with the meat knife and tossed them into the plastic bag with the brain. Then he shook a little salt into his palm and threw that in as well.

Across the other side of the butchering block was a large gas stove upon which sat four blackened pans. They contained various goat parts and were on the boil throughout the day for customers who preferred their meat cooked. Razak took his plastic bag to the stove, tied a knot in the top, and dropped it into the water with the rest. Later they ate it, with spoons, straight from the bag.

The person who ran their section of the butchering block was an Arab named Yosif. He was a large cannonball of a man, with a belly that swung independently from the rest of his body. He was the one they called 'Master', not that he'd ever asked them to address him in such a way but neither had he objected, and the moniker had been handed down through generations of Ghanaians who'd passed through.

Yosif was with them from morning through to evening, bringing fresh heads and taking the meat from the processed ones to sell in the market. Sometimes, if there was specialised butchering required, he would work alongside them. On one occasion, he called Justice over to help with a whole carcass. The goat was lying on its side, still warm.

Yosif slit open its belly just beneath the ribs, reached inside and began pulling handfuls of tubing onto the floor. The stomach came out as well.

The intestine was separated into two piles. Some of it was filled with a moist brown substance, which Yosif squeezed like toothpaste into a sack. He then showed Justice how to roll the intestine inside out, feeding the loose end back through itself, working it along using his index finger. Oily liquid oozed warm and glutinous. It smelled like toilets and drained all over Justice's hands and forearms. It wasn't pleasant but he didn't recoil from the job. It caused no pain and everything else was in the mind.

He plunged a handful of intestine into a bucket of water and kneaded it like a sponge. The animal's stomach still lay on the floor, like a deflated cream football, smooth with a silvery hue. Yosif cut it open, removed some oily handfuls and flipped the whole thing inside out. Justice was surprised to see how the inside had the texture of a towel. He washed that in the bucket too. Then, the clean entrails were packed back inside, re-inflating the stomach and creating a meal which only required boiling water and a pinch of salt.

The other pile of intestines had an altogether more mysterious fate. They were thicker, 'like rope', and after they'd been washed, Yosif took them away in his car, saying they were for export to Europe. 'For hospitals,' he said. 'For transplants.' Justice waited for him to laugh, but he didn't, and whenever he asked the Master about it again, he appeared to become quite cross.

In those first few days, Justice put on a show of enjoying the job, but secretly resolved to improve his situation as soon as he could. He bought a mobile phone, which would ring at 5 a.m. whenever Yosif had work to offer. When there was no call, he spent his time looking for alternative employment. The cola bottling plant was the most appealing. It had clean dry rooms where they processed sugar and mixed together mountains of powdered colours but they asked him for a passport and papers, and Justice left hurriedly in case they called the police. At the smelting company he was captivated by the sight of liquid metal making contact with water and the surge of steam as the amber creaked to black. But when they found out he was only seventeen, they shook their heads and waved him away. Then there was the gas factory, where men lifted heavy blue cylinders onto the backs of trucks. It was way out of town on the Zuwarah road. 'Is this the road that leads to the beach?' Justice asked outside the gates, and it was. The police would be sitting in wait all along here. Zuwarah beach was notorious for people smugglers. If he was seen on the road, they'd think that's where he was heading. They'd arrest him and he'd risk being sent straight back to Qatrun.

Yosif was an honest master, and although the pay was often late, sometimes by several days, it invariably appeared in the end. For a six day week, Justice earned around 50 dinar, (£27). In addition he could make money on the side, buying heads himself for four dinar, then butchering them, and selling his handiwork for four and a half.

Whenever he could, he changed the money into dollars so he had fewer notes, and folded them away in his underpants. 'This way, my body is my bank,' he would say to himself and was certain the others did the same. They would share their food with each other, sleep squeezed so close they could feel each others' breath, squat side by side at the ditch and knee to knee at the mosque, but of savings and money they would never speak. It was safer no one learned the state of your finances.

With Justice having to rise so early for work, he decided he should stay at the tin huts for a while and set about making his room more habitable. He and Saidu salvaged a thick roll of carpet from the tip. It had brown and black swirls, and a rough angular edge which, once installed, rose to knee height in places along the metal walls. Then Justice persuaded the landlord to run a length of wire from an electricity box inside his own home (which itself appeared to be the beneficiary of a tributary from another building) and into theirs. He separated the twist of bare wires and wrapped them in various configurations around the base of a bulb, until it eventually fizzed into action. The installation made theirs one of the most desirable huts in the area.

In Justice's third week, there was a new arrival in the butchering block, a youth who attracted immediate curiosity amongst the other men. The first time Justice saw him, he was being taught how to peel a goat. His appearance was so out of the ordinary it was surprising he'd made it safely to the butchering block at all. Justice wondered why no one had told him how strict the Libyans were about such things.

His hair didn't grow like normal hair but like ropes, stretched across the top of his head in furrows. In one ear he wore a golden coloured stud and around his neck was a thin gold chain. On his feet he had the whitest, cleanest trainers Justice had ever seen and instead of trousers, he was wearing a pair of baggy shorts.

Yosif was trying to demonstrate how to draw the skin away in one piece but the youth was constantly mouthing hellos to the rest of them, or affecting anguished expressions as Yosif wrestled with the hooves. He even patted Yosif on the back and, when the work was done, stood hands on hips, shaking his head in respect, as though he'd never seen such a professionally executed flaying in all his life.

The youth's name was DMX, after the rapper. He was a seventeen-year-old Ghanaian fresh in from the desert. As soon as Yosif left, he was regaling them with a story of how he'd been stopped by two Libyans on his arrival at the Medina. 'They grabbed me by the wrist,' he said. 'And shouted "Mamnuwa!" The earring is an insult.' Justice thought him lucky they'd bothered to explain the problem at all.

'I looked at them and said, "Do you think I'm a black man, eh? You think I'm black?" and they didn't know what to say, so I said, "I'm an American, not a black. Look at these teeth, these are American teeth." And the men, they were laughing so much at the end, we walked and they laughed and told me to be careful, there are men in the Medina with knives.'

After his first day, DMX dispensed with the shoes and the shorts, unless he was visiting the Medina, and most of his time he kept his earring hidden in his pocket. In the workshop, he wore overalls like the rest of them, cut off at the shoulders and rolled at the ankles above his borrowed flip-flops. But his hair remained the same and, as he worked on the goat heads, he picked up on random fragments of conversation, and spun them into nonsensical but passionate raps. The men felt a rare and exotic creature had entered their lives.

On 15 July 2006, six months after he arrived in Tripoli, Justice celebrated his eighteenth birthday. He invited everyone he knew at the market to come to the tin huts that evening, including DMX, his old friend Abu Bakia, Razak, Saidu and several others.

DMX went home first to change and wash, and re-appeared in knee-length shorts with full accessories, 'looking like an American,' they all agreed. Bakia was in his familiar 'London-wear'. Razak and Saidu arrived with plastic bags containing brain and red meat which they'd stashed away at work. They deposited them with Justice and disappeared off to the mosque to wash and pray. Justice prepared two large pans of rice, set them to boil on the stove, and then headed off to join the rest.

When they returned, several others had gathered, some in their work dungarees, or sandals and shorts. They drank cans of cola and Mashrud mineral drink and Justice handed out bayrush cakes from his favourite stall. Most of the men had been sleeping outside since the summer began, so there was a selection of mats and mattresses for people to choose from. Justice was in charge of cooking; meat stew with plenty of tomatoes, onions and some herbs he'd picked up at the market. At some stage a cassette player was produced, from which the front flap had long-since been broken and which was rigged up to the landlord's electricity supply. They listened to Ghanaian music as the light around them faded and the heat hung in the air.

'How long before you go?' whispered Razak to DMX.

DMX glanced behind him, 'Who goes where?'

'Come on, I heard you nearly had the money when you arrived, that was months ago, you must have it by now.'

DMX smiled and shrugged his shoulders. 'I may have the money but I haven't been called to come.'

'Even the wisest men don't always choose lamp-lampa,' said Razak. 'You have family. You are better for them at home than at the bottom of the water.'

'I never said I was going,' said DMX.

'That's good. If you say you're going and an Arab finds out, he might tell the police,' said Razak. 'Either that or he might come to your house and steal all your money. You should tell one person you trust, in case something goes wrong, but no one else should know, until you're there.'

The other men had stopped talking now, and listened instead to Razak.

'When you have chosen that person, the one you trust, leave your mobile phone number with them. Leave your parents' address too. If you have a photo, well that is good. It means we can send it back to your home. If your mother and father had no pictures of you before, they can look at it and pray.'

Bakia rose slowly to his feet, like he was carrying an extra person, and wandered over to the cassette player, pretending to fiddle with the volume.

'Bakia's been here for more than a year,' said Justice. 'He is probably close. What about you Razak, how long have you been waiting?'

Razak blew a line in the air, 'A long time. Many years I've been here.'

They waited for him to fill the gap.

'I have seen many people come through here. Many people arrive and leave. I have had many friends. Friends who shared food like this,' he spoke so lightly, Bakia had to turn the volume down so he could catch what came next. 'In my book, I have telephone numbers and names. Many of them. I call them when they are gone. Sometimes, nothing. I try them again a week later. Still nothing. I have lost many friends. Many. Maybe hundreds.'

It was the height of the crossing season and a kind of fever had settled over Gurji. Each day, it seemed, there were stories of men vanishing from their beds, violent storms way out on the Mediterranean, men battling through high seas, capsizes, safe arrivals, bodies washed up on beaches. When Justice turned up for football, some of the regular faces had gone, new ones had arrived. The community was in flux. Bakia had become an increasingly distant figure, still praying at the mosque and eating with the others, but in his mind he'd already gone. Saidu was mysteriously silent about whether he intended to sail or not. DMX had been in several more scrapes at the Medina and had managed to wriggle out of each, returning home with ever more outlandish tales. Razak was in contact with several men who'd made it to the other side and was constantly relaying the news back into the community.

A couple of days after his birthday, Justice made an announcement at the tin huts. He was giving up and returning to Ghana.

Chapter Five

If he told them the truth, wicked things could happen. Some day soon, he might wake up in the morning and find one of his legs had grown big and fat, and when he tried to lift it, it would lie on the mattress like wet bread. He would never walk again, and his leg would be so swollen he'd never raise himself from the floor. What about his head? What if it was his head that swelled up and the rest of his body was too weak to lift it, a doll's body with a giant's head. Then he would certainly not be able to leave the house. How could he know who was prepared to use black medicine, or the spells of a fetish priest on someone trying to earn extra money?

There were other risks too. What if some of the men had Libyan friends with weapons? They might find him and hurt him for what he was about to do. Even the Ghanaians who were his friends, they might do the same. So he'd lied. He could call it nothing else.

As he sat on the bus, he reassured himself with the Koran: '*Remember when Joseph said to his father, "Oh my father! Verily I saw in a dream eleven stars and the sun and the moon, I saw them prostrating themselves to me." He, the father, said, "Oh my son! Relate not your vision to your brothers, lest they arrange a plot against you . . ."*'

'*. . . Arrange a plot against you*', it was settled then. The story he gave was the safest. What he was really planning was between him and his God.

The minibus travelled east out of Tripoli. There were abandoned diggers and concrete mixers, bottle-shaped palms dotting the road, bleached Peugeot vans racing tractors from the lights, traders selling marble slabs the size of billiard tables. An hour later, there was only sand, tumbling cacti and a narrow strip of asphalt across the plain.

It was only a short drive to where he was going, perhaps six hours. He had with him a sports bag containing two pairs of trousers, a shirt, a pair of sandals, and some biscuits for the journey. His mobile phone was in his trouser pocket and his money was in its normal place.

Justice had been given a number to call, which he did on arrival, and was instructed to make his way to an area on the outskirts of town. When he arrived at a three-storey sand-coloured building, he climbed the stairs and the door was opened by a young Ghanaian man, who invited Justice inside.

The apartment was pleasantly furnished with a settee and television set, and a number of mattresses leaning against the walls. Justice looked at the smooth tiled floor. Through a doorway he could see a sink with silver-coloured taps and next to it a white metal cooker. The windows were open and a slight breeze blew through the apartment. 'There are five of us here,' said the man who opened the door. 'We have a spare place to sleep which you are welcome to. How long will you stay?'

'I don't know,' he said. 'Maybe as long as they will have me, if they take me at all.'

The next day he was outside a pair of tall metal gates, far from the houses and office blocks. The gates and the silver buildings beyond were covered in a film of white dust. It floated in the air, as fine as smoke, and each passing lorry churned more of it into the sky, so it seemed it would never come down.

The buildings themselves were a labyrinth of pipes, helter-skeltering down the sides, weaving from one structure to another, some of them running in tight unison for a while, then fanning out and plunging beneath the ground, finger thin and fat enough to crawl through. There were rocks riding along conveyor belts high in the sky, and stairways curling around the outside of buildings. At the centre of it all was a thick cylindrical tower from which drifted a plume of pure white smoke sitting almost motionless against the backdrop of blue sky.

The factory was in Libya's third city, Misratah, a prosperous business centre with angular white architecture, Arabesque arches, wide boulevards fringed with palms and rows of shrubs shaved into dramatic cubes. At night the grass roundabouts and parks became floodlit lime. To its south and west were sandy plains, to its north and east, the Mediterranean. But there was no network for crossing to Europe from here and that was not why he came.

His job was lifting bags of cement onto the backs of trucks. As he'd been promised, it was better than the butchering block – no darkness, no fire, no blood. He was outside most of the time and only had to go into the packing room to pick up sacks. The downside was the dust which he continued to cough out of his lungs for several days after he left. The pay was fifteen dinar a day (around £8), which was half as much again as he received in Gurji.

If anyone discovered he was earning more money, and for doing an easier job, then that was when the juju might begin. Coming here, breaking from the crowd, finding an easier path, it might seem disloyal to some. They were all supposed to move along together. Shortcuts, even if they disadvantaged no one, were a form of cheating. He was sure Razak wouldn't feel that way, nor DMX, nor Bakia, but it only needed one man with a dead chicken and some carefully crafted words to invoke the spirits.

Whilst in Misratah, there was an event which would stay with Justice for some time. Usually, Libyan television showed speeches from Gaddafi, two to three hours long, and then repeated them the following day, but on one occasion, there were a series of special reports, one of which caught his eye. The item began with shots of a sandy beach of such length and breadth it appeared the desert ran straight into the sea. There was a rusting children's climbing frame, disused swings, and the occasional wicker screen shredded by the wind, but there were no cars, no trees, no houses, and the spray from the waves threw the whole scene out of focus.

Then, the camera picked out a bundle of clothes. It was

some way down the beach, within the wash of the more reachy waves, but too sodden to be shifted any further. The current had sucked the sand from beneath so it lay low in a hollow. As the camera moved closer, Justice could make out what it was. The red fleece had been pulled up over the chest to expose a tightly inflated belly. Instead of skin, it seemed to be shaped from the same tissue as inside the goat's stomach, thick towelling all the way through. The head was turned away from the camera but Justice could see the black in the skin had been bleached into nicotine yellow. A police vehicle stood nearby, waiting on the sand.

Then, there was a shot of a whole line of bodies, all with the same sickeningly swollen bellies. A man in uniform stood nearby. He pointed out to sea and then back again. He was explaining that the attempt couldn't have made it far off the coast, or they wouldn't have washed back like this. 'We're stepping up efforts,' he said, 'to stop these things from happening. Our patrols are catching them and if they don't, then the sea will.'

Justice spent ten weeks in Misratah before returning to Tripoli and to the tin huts. If he managed to keep his legs from turning to bread, the extra money at the cement works should mean he could set out for Europe early in the new season.

It was the end of September when he arrived back in Gurji and it was like the breath had been beaten out of the place. Along the coast road, the wind tugged at flags and spat the tops off waves. The queue of boats in the harbour was shorter now and froth lines stretched out behind them bending westwards in the current.

The taps outside the mosque were quiet and in the work-shops, the banter subdued. Those who'd still not received the call knew they would have to wait until next spring. Those whose names were on the list were constantly fretful, knowing the window of opportunity was narrowing and that, as winter approached, the organisers were prepared to take more risks with the weather. There was a backlog to clear and even if the skies were heavy with thunder, they'd send the boats to sea knowing that, if the trip failed, no one was going to return to complain.

When Justice arrived at the door of his old room, it was locked.

'You looking for somewhere to stay?' an unfamiliar face appeared from a neighbouring hut. 'The landlord, he lives in the room across there, but he's out now.'

'I was living here before,' said Justice, pointing to the metal door.

'Okay, but that room is full now.'

'Saidu will find room, even if I have to lie with him on his own mattress.'

'Saidu?' replied the man. 'Saidu has gone.'

A month before, Saidu had moved away. He had told the others he'd had enough of butchering and was off to find work at another market. Justice never saw him again. Instead he moved into a larger hut, opposite the last and three doors down. The front of it was tin and so was the door, but the side walls and the back were made from brick. The room was home to five men, and Justice's arrival made it six. It was adjoining the landlord's room, and there was a small open window at the top of one wall from which, if you stood on a box, you could see right through to him. The window was used to run two electrical wires from the landlord's supply, one into a bulb, the other into a television set.

The first Justice learned of the mystery was from a Ghanaian working in the market. A man had appeared in Gurji almost incoherent with distress. He said he'd been in the sea, swimming for hours, he wasn't sure how many, but he'd found himself washed up on a beach many miles from Tripoli. He was scared they were going to catch him, the police that is, scared they'd spotted him leaving the water. He thought the rest were dead, he wasn't sure, but he didn't think they could swim and when the boat had gone down there was nothing left to hang onto. It was a 'balloon boat', he said, full of air, and when they were out on the ocean, it had burst.

That was all the Ghanaian knew. The whereabouts of the distressed man were unclear. Some said he was hiding in a hut, humbled and scared, like he'd seen his God. Others said he'd fled back across the desert saying if he set eyes on the water again he would surely die.

The story of the 'balloon boat' was soon the talk of Gurji. Normally, information seeped back via men like Razak, men who would receive phone calls after a boat had landed on the other side. The unsuccessful crossings were different. It was the silence which told of their fate. After a fortnight without a call, there'd be some anxiety, but the men knew so little of the sea, they would wait another two weeks before guessing the boat had gone down. For parents and families the wait was longer. They might not know their son, or husband, had any intention of attempting the crossing. For them it could be months or years before they understood the silence. Even then, they might suspect it was disease that took him, or dehydration whilst crossing the desert, or perhaps a beating by border guards. How could they ever know it was the sea?

Around Gurji, stories of the dead were a kind of currency, passed from one man to the next, swapped around, translated, and then fed back into the system. The truth was fluid, limited only by their collective imagination. There was no reason to disbelieve stories of sea serpents, because the sea itself was relatively new. Its properties were a mystery to those about to cross it. Perhaps waves could grow large enough to sweep away a boat. Perhaps the bottom was as deep as the tallest mountain. Perhaps the water wasn't like water from the well but a kind of poison which would make your stomach burn and your brain go cold. And so they lived in a world where the laws of nature were still being created. Although it meant the men of Gurji conjured many terrible images of ways in which they might die, it also gave them hope that in the magical wilderness of the sea there would be benevolent forces; forces they didn't understand but which would counterbalance the evil and in the end ensure their salvation.

Razak himself had once unwittingly contributed to the myths of the crossing.

Razak had died. The man who'd advised so many and waited for so long, had, in the end, chosen the wrong moment. He'd perished with twenty or so others, shortly after setting sail from Zuwarah Beach. A body had been washed up, and from that, the people smugglers had managed to identify several of the men on board. One of them was Razak.

The news circulated quickly around Gurji. 'Razak? Why would God take him? He had done only good.' In the market they laid down their buckets and wheelbarrows and stood in quiet bewilderment. 'Did he leave a picture for his mother? Who will phone her?' They were numb with the news, and some even prayed to his spirit to ask it what they should do.

When the news reached Razak he smiled sadly, and spent the next few days surprising his friends with appearances around the market. Razak had indeed died, but it was another Razak, based in a different part of town. The one from the butchering shops of Gurji was still alive.

The true number of dead on the crossing, and hence the real risk for anyone about to try it, was unknown. Even the international agencies which monitor the route have little reliable evidence. Its secretive and illicit nature means no one knows for sure.

For the men of Gurji, death was rarely a sudden event. It didn't arrive by telephone or fax or email, but gradually settled over them like the close of day. They were never sure when the light had begun to fade but they knew when it had gone.

When Justice returned to the butchering block after his time away, there were whistled greetings and many questions. 'How was Ghana my friend? . . . Back so soon? . . . Your family must be sad . . . Maybe his family doesn't want him!'

114

Among the familiar faces was DMX, surrounded by dismantled goat heads, tools poised like drumsticks. It was good to see him. Justice had thought he might have already left, but there he was, dungarees styled into shorts, and a baseball cap covering his braided hair. Razak was there too, watching quietly from behind his bench.

'In Ghana life is hard,' Justice said. 'There is nothing to stay for.' He left it at that.

The men knew not to reach into each others' business. The talk turned to the 'balloon boat'. They'd heard about the survivor, that there was just one, that the others were all dead. But no one was sure who'd been on board. There were plenty of unaccounted absences around Gurji at the time, there always were. It didn't mean any of them had been aboard that particular boat.

It was whilst Justice was walking back through the market that the news reached him. It came from a Ghanaian youth who lived with a different group, on the other side of town.

'Bakia was in the balloon boat,' he said. That was it. Nothing else. Justice didn't ask any questions. He just thanked the man and set off back to the tin huts.

The bodies were washed up on Zuwarah Beach, where they were lined up in the sand, and filmed for Libyan television. They were carrying no paperwork, nothing that could identify them. That's how it normally was. If they had made it to Europe, they could have claimed to be from wherever they chose – Liberia perhaps or Sudan, maximising their chances of political asylum and ensuring they could stay, at least whilst their stories were investigated.

There's a sandy hillside on the Gergaresh Road in Tripoli

which overlooks the sea. It's lined with grey and cream cement slabs and coffin-shaped boxes. These are the graves of the unknown dead, the Africans washed up at sea. Their headstones are often just a single breezeblock. Some have none at all. There are so many 'unknowns' buried in the Sidi Hamed graveyard, they've run out of space. This is where Abu Bakia lies, near to an orange and white fence by the sea, somewhere between where he came from and where he was heading. After the burial, Razak asked Justice who should tell the parents.

Justice said, 'Not now, we should wait a while.' Some days later when he'd worked up the courage, he called Alhaji himself. 'Your son is dead,' he said. 'He died at sea. He was in a balloon boat and it burst.' There were no words in response. 'Just a gush,' said Justice.

Alhaji has four photographs of his son, Abu Bakia. One is from his Ghanaian identity card. The others are all from Tripoli. They're grainy, overexposed, worn in places. There's a group shot with Bakia smiling confidently at the camera, bulky and tall, wearing a cream-coloured fleece and woollen hat like he's off on a walking weekend. In another he's with a young Arab man in the same location. It appears to be some kind of lock-up garage with mattresses in the background and a bed frame. Then there's a picture that's been shot with more care. Bakia is posing outside on a street. He's wearing a denim jacket with faded pockets and a design in gold on his back. On his head is a black baseball cap. He has a gold-coloured band around one wrist. The scene could be New York, London or Rome. Bakia isn't looking into the camera. He's staring into the distance, his hands are clasped and he's leaning against a white Mercedes. And for a moment it's his, a white Mercedes on a sunny day, a life of ease and plenty captured on a postcard.

It was evening in Green Square and the locals were queuing to have their picture taken with a baby antelope. Its owner had it tethered securely with a chain, and whilst the women crouched just outside its reach, the men crowded it and then scattered as the animal repeatedly lowered its head and charged. Nearby youngsters posed on tangerine- and strawberry-coloured Harley Davidsons, or on swings wreathed with plastic flowers. A boy, no older than ten, was charging around on a mini-bike, buzzing between the pedestrians, cheered on by his friends. It was the busiest time of the day and on the grass, families picnicked in a haze of sweet barbecue.

Justice and DMX wandered through the crowds, crossed the blocked road at the other side, and headed towards the harbour. They'd sat on the bench before. It was positioned on a strip of parched grass where children ate ice cream and open top carriages paused to take in the sea. Behind it were the mediaeval walls of the Medina, in front the Mediterranean. The harbour wall stretched out in a crescent to the east, merchant boats tucked in its lee. The names written across their hulls were unfamiliar and exotic: 'Valetta', 'Rotterdam', and 'Naples'.

Justice thought the boats looked as tall and solid as buildings. A crane was plucking orange-coloured containers from one of the decks and stacking them like bricks on the quayside.

'People can sleep in them, they have beds,' he said. 'When they eat, they have tables.' Another boat was passing around the tip of the harbour, from the rough water to the calm. 'When the waves hit them, the boats don't move,' Justice said.

Bakia's drowning had not dimmed their desire, these deaths never did. Those who perished were viewed as men lost in action and for the rest the campaign was still underway. They couldn't start questioning its merits. They needed to push on. Only what was ahead was worth living for. There were those who made it, those who died trying, and those who remained at home. Only one category was judged a failure.

A narrow metal walkway was being lowered from one of the boats. A sailor ran to the bottom to secure it and then disappeared back on board. Moments later, a line of men sauntered down onto the quayside, and onto a waiting bus.

'They come here today, Europe tomorrow, maybe next week America. The boat is so high. Look at it. How can the waves ever reach them?' DMX nodded as Justice continued, 'It can take a hundred containers and it still won't sink. Look how many people are coming from it. Another passenger would not be a problem.'

DMX turned to him and began to laugh. 'Hey, you want to be with the Europeans? You think they'll sell you a ticket?'

Justice was undeterred. This was his plan: he would approach a Westerner in Green Square and offer them all his dollars to be hidden in a cabin. Because they were foreigners, they were unlikely to take him to the police. The worst that could happen is for them to run off with his money. So, he would refuse to hand it over, until he was curled safely in the dark beneath their bunk and the Medina walls were sliding away behind him. That would have to be the agreement. In didn't matter where in Europe it was sailing to. Hopefully it would be England, but if not, at least he'd be on the right continent. And they'd never ask for passports at the other side, because these were Europeans arriving home, so there'd be no guards asking for paperwork or anything like that. He'd just disembark with the others and whilst they were climbing into their cars, he'd persuade someone to give him a lift to London.

'Yes, but can you make yourself invisible?' said DMX. 'How do you get on the boat? Do you hide in someone's bags?'

'No one will ask questions,' said Justice. 'How can they remember who gets on and who gets off? There are too many people. I will just climb on board with the rest of the passengers.'

The two men remained on the bench until darkness fell and the water looked like warm oil. Somewhere out there, if he squinted, Justice imagined he could see lights. It was said a tiny island lay off the coast, he wasn't sure in which direction but it was supposed to be within reach of a small boat. Everyone doing lampa-lampa talked about it, but whether it really existed, he wasn't certain. It was said the island was filled with Europeans, that there were cars and brick houses and that the women lay on the sand in their underwear. If you could make it there, they would take you to England or Italy or Spain and you would find work and be happy. But the island was said to be small and the currents unpredictable, and if you missed it you might drift on, to another island where no one would ever choose to go.

The other island was a little further away, and you wouldn't know you were near it until the men came in their boats to capture you. They too were white but when they took you to their island, they would put you in cages. There would be no escape from these cages and even when they released you, your freedom would be a small island from which you couldn't leave.

'It won't work,' whispered Razak the following day. He had a length of rubber tubing looped over his arm which fed the gas into his blow torch and which he kept repositioning to try to achieve a more even flow. 'I don't want to upset you my friend but you are thinking white people are the same as blacks.' His blow torch shrank to the strength of a candle, coughed a couple of times and then returned with a ferocity that took them both by surprise. 'If you ask a black man to take you in his cabin, he would consider how much room he had, and if there was space enough for two, he would agree. You could pay him very little money indeed and he would be content.'

Razak laid the flame down and was absent-mindedly breaking flesh from the goat's cheek, and patting it into a pile on the bench. 'White men are different. Even if they had a spare bed in their cabin, they would prefer it to be empty than have Justice Amin lying there. Even if it was one of their own, another white man, they would not give that space to anyone. If you offer them money, they already have money. Your money will be too little, no matter how much you have. Believe me, I have thought of this plan. Some people, they have even tried. But no one has ever made it work.'

Justice signalled for him to stop talking. Another group of workers was settling down to a fresh barrow of heads on the bench opposite and Justice didn't want them to overhear. 'What will you do when you reach the other side?' asked Justice.

'Oh, I think butchering would be good for me,' replied Razak, concentrating on the stubborn pieces of black meat around the jaw. 'I could skin heads in Italy or England or wherever they needed me, and I would carry on until my mother had enough money so she would never have to worry again.'

Razak hadn't told anyone, but his mother was the real reason he'd never made the crossing. He'd left Ghana when he was twenty-eight years old with plans to become a professional footballer. The idea was to secure a trial in Italy or England and become the next Michael Essien. He'd seen on television how much money the man was being paid. Razak was now thirty-six, but he still thought it possible. If only he could persuade his mother it was the right thing to do. But she was firm. 'Don't go across the water,' she said to him. 'You are my only son. Without you there will be no grandchildren.'

It had become their ritual to play football after prayers almost every night of the week. There would be several matches underway simultaneously – five-a-side, fifteen-a-side, pitches that overlapped, players switching teams, players switching games. These were hectic, physical games where the result was less important than personal glory.

Razak's gentle deference evaporated on the pitch, and was replaced with a fiery ruthlessness which, when combined with his 6'2" frame, made him a player to be avoided. DMX was bullish, unpredictable, prone to ball-trickery and futile long-distance shots, but he had pace and confused the opposition by simultaneously playing in every position on the pitch. Justice was always in goal. He was one of the shortest players in the team but strong like a tree and whenever the mood took him, he would charge down the pitch and assist with the attack. A newcomer called Atiku often played too. He was tall and rubbery, and ran everywhere both on and off the pitch. Atiku had arrived in Gurji late in the season, after working outside town sewing clothes. Even his trademark 'Van Dutch' woollen hat was really his own work. He was on his way to Europe to be a fashion designer.

It was during these games that a number of local men began appearing and playing alongside them. 'They are the stone throwers and the thieves,' several of the migrants warned. 'Their friends will steal from our rooms whilst we play.'

But Justice argued they should be invited to join in: the landlord from the tin huts – he had been generous with his electricity; the owner of the 'phone home' shop – he always offered them sweet mint tea. 'Why exclude them because of what others have done?' asked Justice. 'We cannot blame them for their brothers.'

However, many of the locals scorned the idea too and the men continued to play their separate games. Change came about in a curious way. One evening they were playing under the floodlights of the Medina. It was a hot night. Residents had flung open their windows in the tower blocks, the car-washing boys (mainly Nigerians) had packed up work early and were lounging beside the pitch. Even the dust seemed to radiate heat.

During a break in play Justice slipped down an alleyway to relieve himself. As he stood against the wall, one of the Libyans appeared. He was a large fat man in his mid-twenties who Justice recognised as a stone thrower. He'd once driven his pick-up at a group of migrants and slammed on the brakes just short of them. They'd felt like beating him, but instead they'd apologised for being in his way.

The Libyan positioned himself further up the alleyway and leaned into the wall. Soon, a line of urine meandered down to where Justice stood. He lifted his feet to let it go by. When he'd finished, and was walking past the wet patch he noticed something, and called back up the road to the overweight Libyan. 'Look,' he said, 'cockroaches.'

They'd crawled from beneath a stone and where running around busily in the damp. 'Too much sugar,' said Justice. 'That is why the cockroaches are here. They enjoy the sweet-ness.' The Libyan watched as more of them tumbled down the wall. 'You should go and see a doctor,' said Justice.

A few days later, the Libyan came to find Justice at the pitches near to the Medina. 'You are a good man,' he said. 'I have been for tests. They gave me tablets. The doctor told me I am diabetic.'

Over the months, relations between the two sides mellowed, and they began a series of internationals: Ghana vs Libya. Some of the Arabs would even lend the migrants kit. Justice and the others wanted the lime green colours of Al 'Ahly. It was the Tripoli team Gaddafi's son once played for. He'd made sympathetic speeches about migrants and so it was Al 'Ahly they supported. But the Libyans teased them by always giving them red and white stripes. That was the colour of Gaddafi's team.

Along the top of the Medina ran an ancient walkway, broad and walled on either side and continuing for almost its entire length. One side dropped away sheer to the coast road, dwarfing the palm trees beneath which barely reached its midpoint. On the other, the buildings were so dense it seemed there was no floor, just flat roofs littered with aerials and pieces of broken furniture. Along the outer edge were battlements where cannon holes looked out over the sea. Most were packed with cola cans and cigarette packets. Every now and then a set of stone steps descended from the walkway down into the relative cool. It was the route Justice took to the post office at the far end of the Medina.

'So, the money is small, but the journey is safe, I promise you,' the voice came from behind a low wall. 'These people, they have more success than anyone. And there is no worry about getting caught. Seriously. The police are working with them. I didn't believe it at first, but I've seen it myself.'

Justice repositioned himself slightly to see who was talking but pretended his ears were elsewhere. It was an African, a Ghanaian, probably in his mid-twenties, dressed in clean white training shoes, western-style jeans, a white long-sleeved shirt and a pair of orange-tinted sunglasses which kept sliding down his nose.

'Yes, yes, lampa-lampa. These men, I have known them for a long time. You can trust them. If people were dying in their boats, I wouldn't be working with them.' The man was interrupted on his mobile for a moment and then resumed. 'The boats they use are the best in Zuwarah. They're made of plastic like the fishermen use. You can see how far they sail. If they weren't safe, the fishermen wouldn't use them.'

'How much?' asked the other voice.

'A thousand dollars. And it's a good price, I promise you. If you wait too long, the lists will fill up and the price will double. Do you have the money?'

The other man was a teenager who looked like he'd come straight from the market. He was leaning against the wall with his back to Justice, facing the man in the orange sunglasses. 'I don't know if I have the money. It's a lot,' he said and made as if to walk away.

'Not a lot, and we have something special. No one else in Zuwarah can offer such a thing.'

The teenager was curious, and settled back against the wall.

'You know the metal boats,' continued the man in the orange glasses. 'The ones the Westerners use? We have one. There is no way we can bring it to the beach, because it would be spotted, and anyway the sea is too shallow. These boats need deep water. So we keep it far out. You and your friends, we put you in a small plastic boat, and we sail you out to meet it. When you arrive, you board the metal boat, and from there you go to Europe.'

Connection men are chosen for their persuasive sales-manship. They usually operate solely within their own community, Ghanaian to Ghanaian, Ivorian to Ivorian, and are seen as privileged individuals, well-rewarded by the

Libyan organisers for whom they are the only link into African neighbourhoods. They are recruited whilst they themselves are planning to make the crossing, often by another connection man who has made enough money and whose thoughts are turning towards home. It's believed they take a 10 per cent cut of the money they bring in. If that's true, it's far more than they would have earned had they sailed to Europe.

For the people-smugglers to have access to a metal boat was something Justice had not come across before. No one had spoken of such a thing in Gurji, but perhaps he shouldn't be surprised. These smugglers had contacts at the highest levels and were always trying to outdo their competitors with larger vessels or faster engines. It made sense they should have acquired the biggest boat they could find. After all, it meant more space for migrants, and therefore more profit for the smugglers. It would suit Justice well, reducing the risk of sinking, but also making the arrival in port less suspicious. A metal ship would be assumed official, and perhaps there would even be Europeans on board, with whom Justice might mingle as they disembarked.

The Ghanaian with the sunglasses had produced his mobile phone again, and was this time carefully punching in the contact number of the teenager, who shook his hand and wandered back into the Medina. 'Remember,' he shouted after him. 'Tell your friends they can come too. Same deal. I will be here tomorrow.'

Justice climbed down from the wall and approached the connection man. 'You do lampa-lampa brother?' he asked, trying to appear casual. He could see now the man was younger than he'd first thought, perhaps no more than twenty. He had a different look from the Ghanaians in the market. The white shirt had buttons down the front, like a man from England – 'London-wear' thought Justice – and both that and his trousers were without stains. His face shone with good health and self-confidence and he reached out a welcoming hand, which Justice took with some relief.

The conversation began badly. Justice wanted to know his name but the man insisted he wouldn't give it. 'You must understand, if I give you my name and you are arrested on Zuwarah road, the policemen, they will force it out of you. If I don't tell you, then you can't be tempted.'

Justice accepted the explanation, and the conversation shifted to the metal boat. 'Where did it come from?' asked Justice.

'No one says. Maybe it used to be like a ferry, for taking people across the sea. There are rooms, that's what they tell me, and a captain who steers it and will take it to Italy.'

'So, you haven't seen it?'

'Listen brother, beware, there are others who will take your money and you will never see a boat. I know these organisers, they have no reason to lie.'

Justice was told he wouldn't have to pay until arrival at the beach but the reality was that these organisers, like any others, could take his money and provide nothing in return. There were stories of men arriving at Zuwarah and being killed by the smugglers before they even saw a boat. It wasn't far-fetched. Everyone would assume they'd simply gone the way of so many others. Whether they were murdered on the sand or drowned at sea it didn't really matter to the organisers, either way they got their money.

Then again, the metal boat in the harbour carried a risk too. Assuming he could rely on a European for help, there was still a real possibility he would be caught whilst boarding. That would mean an indefinite stay at somewhere like Qatrun, where the guards would no doubt be delighted to welcome back an escapee.

'I have the money,' said Justice. 'When will I be called to come?'

'In eight weeks the weather will ease,' the man said shaking Justice's hand once again. 'I will call you then and tell you when the boat is ready. After that, it is up to the Libyans. When they say it's time, you must come.'

As the bus drove back along the coast road to Gurji, Justice comforted himself with the thought that if he changed his mind, he could ignore the calls from the man with the orange sunglasses and choose a different route to Europe.

Chapter Six

DMX had left. He'd told no one. The men from his hut said they'd woken to find his mattress empty, his possessions gone.

'Even if you die in a fire in a house, or when your house breaks in an earthquake, the pain cannot be equal,' Justice said. 'When your boat is gone, even if you can swim in the sea, you will drink the water and become so heavy that you can no longer float.'

After two weeks without hearing a word, Justice realised with sadness that his anxiety over the fate of DMX was starting to subside, that he was gently releasing his old friend.

'The pain is bad when the sea takes them but there will be no punishment on the other side. All of them will wake up again,' he said.

Justice was spending more time at the internet café near to the mosque. It was on the side of the square most exposed to the wind, where the unfortunate shopkeepers needed to spray the ground to keep the powder sand at bay. From the outside, the building appeared to be an abandoned shop. Its front window was weathered like an old Coke bottle, frosted by the sun and sand, then coated in layers of sugary grime. The stickers on the inside showed cowboys with cigarettes, European footballers in mid-strike, verses of the Koran in Disney writing. Around the sills, palm green paint bubbled from the woodwork. The door was set on springs, so to enter was like barging into a spaghetti western.

Inside there were booths where customers, mainly African migrants, phoned home or browsed the internet. It was there, in the spring of 2007 that Justice began following world events with a new eye, acclimatising himself to the outside. He read about the kidnap of BBC journalist Alan Johnson, the disappearance of Madeleine McCann, the Virginia Tech massacre, events that no longer seemed so far away. He studied the English premiership, and followed the match live as Manchester United beat Roma 7–1 in the Champions League. He was preparing the ground, making sure that by the time he arrived he would no longer be a stranger.

In early April he arrived at the internet café to make an important phone call to his brother Issah. In the summer the shop became a noisy social club, due to its ancient but highly effective air conditioning unit which was perpetually switched to maximum. It was fixed high on a wall and the men would gather beneath it, rubbing their shaved heads and stretching their arms upwards like they were bathing in a cool shower. Justice sat on a table by himself and made the call to Ghana.

'I have a crossing to Europe,' he told Issah. 'I am not sure when the day will come but it will come soon.'

In April 2007, the heat was enough to toast the juice from the bunched coriander and crack the glaze on tomatoes. The barrow boys slouched beneath the blue tarpaulin, sipping mineral water and eating nuts. Traders sold their wares straight from the back of Japanese jeeps, or propped sheeted cardboard beneath their windscreen and slept. Then, three weeks after he'd vanished, DMX reappeared with as little fuss as when he'd left. He wandered into the market, slightly thinner, a little sheepish perhaps, but still with his hair braided and his swagger intact.

'The men picked me up in the Medina and took me to Zuwarah Beach,' he told his friends that evening. 'There is a small house there and we stayed.'

'We wanted to leave on the first night. That is what we had prepared for. But the wind was strong and the Libyans told us the waves were so high the boat wouldn't reach beyond them.'

'Where was the boat?' asked Razak. 'Did they show you the boat you would sail in?'

'No, we never saw it. There was a tractor outside the house, like a farmer would use, but that is all.' Someone passed a plate of rice and stew to DMX but it sat untouched on his lap as he continued. 'The next day, the wind had become stronger and again the Libyans said we could not leave. We had not eaten since before we arrived, so we asked if we could go and buy food from a village nearby. They said we couldn't because the police would be suspicious if they saw Africans in the area. They said we should give them money and they would go on our behalf. But we had already paid them for the journey and most of us had nothing left.' The men ate and listened in silence. 'After two weeks, I had still not eaten, apart from some biscuits they gave us. I spent all day lying on the floor. I was too weak for the crossing, I knew I was. So I returned to Gurji.'

No one asked why the Libyans allowed him to leave, they assumed DMX wise-cracked his way out of it. The other men out on Zuwarah, around thirty of them, had remained at the house near the beach. Within days news reached Gurji of their fate. The weather had calmed the day after DMX returned to town. The sea was smooth, the wind gentle and the boat was launched that very night. A week later the men had spotted land for the first time and headed straight for it. They'd been met by a rescue boat which escorted them to a place they discovered was called Sicily. It was from there one of them phoned DMX to share the good news. They'd arrived safely without a single loss of life.

That was his boat, his crossing. He could have been on a train now dashing through the Italian countryside and heading for England, or choosing an apartment with carpets and internal stairs like he'd seen on television. Those men would be in jobs by now, sending money home. He should be happy for them. How would he have felt if they'd perished? Despair at the loss of so many, or relief he wasn't on board? The path he'd followed from Ghana led to Gurji, to that connection man, to Zuwarah and that boat, and now he recognised God had been leading him always to safety.

DMX never fully returned to the life he'd led before. On the occasions he visited the butchering block he appeared preoccupied. The boisterousness, the rapping, the wheel-barrow races, all had gone. Now he wafted around between the football pitch and the market without properly reaching either. One boat with his name on it had arrived safely in Europe. What were the chances of a second doing the same?

When he vanished again in early May 2007, up to five boatfuls a night were said to be leaving Zuwarah Beach. The old guard were on the move, the newcomers were arriving daily, emerging from the desert to find vacated rooms, abandoned gas ovens, stained overalls drying on the metal rooftops. This time DMX did make it into a boat. But neither he, nor any of the others on board were ever heard from again.

It was a Friday evening after Maghreb prayer when it finally happened. Justice put the water on the fire, ran to the mosque, and returned to find it simmering away in the large tin pan. He added some vegetable powder until it firmed up and then stirred it until the texture was some-where between soup and porridge. Then he added a little goat meat. He'd not eaten since the previous evening and fully intended a larger portion for himself than for any of the others. His mobile rang before he'd had chance to start serving.

'This night it should be possible,' it was the voice of the man in the orange sunglasses. Justice could tell he was in a hurry. 'We can offer a price of 500 dollars but I need to know now.' It was a good deal. Some gangs charged three times that. Justice agreed. This was his season. He wasn't prepared to wait any longer. 'The weather is good, the ship is available. You should prepare to travel.' The instructions came at him so quickly Justice was worried he'd missed some crucial points.

As soon as he put the phone down, he raised himself from the fire, and walked slowly back towards his room. Even with the door wide open, the air sat still, gently cooking the assorted clothes and shoes. He began packing the sportsbag he'd bought at Friday Market. It was red with a shoulder strap. On its side was written 'Manchester United' with a picture of Wayne Rooney, his fist punching the air in celebration of a goal. Into it Justice placed a single pair of trousers, a T-shirt, a small notebook with contact numbers and addresses and his Koran.

He slung the bag over his shoulder, and left the hut at seven o'clock. His friends were still eating daggie around the fire. 'I will be back,' he said and then dipped in a spoon, drew out several pieces of meat and filled his mouth before setting off down the dust path, through the plastic crates stacked at the entrance to the cul-de-sac, and across the empty marketplace towards the bus stop.

It was the evening of 22 May 2007, almost two years since Justice had left his uncle's hut in Effiakuma. The temperature in Tripoli that day was a little above 20°C, around average for the time of year. The air was humid and there was quite a breeze, enough to rustle the palm trees around the Medina and ripple the fountain in Green Square. Out at Zuwarah, conditions were more severe. The temperature was similar to that in town but the wind was gusting up to forty miles an hour, enough to make the palm trees sway and the wind whistle through the telegraph wires. At sea, the water was heaping up on itself, the waves churning white streaks in the direction of the wind.

Justice disembarked from the bus at the interchange just after eight o'clock. The hawkers had cleared the pavements, the businessmen had retired to the columned squares to smoke mint and apple hubbabubba and play draughts. Yellow floodlights were splashed across the Arabesque arch of the Corinthia Hotel and guests were congregating on the lower floor terrace for dinner.

Justice headed straight for the main entrance to the Medina and followed its familiar alleyways to the north side and the shops. He needed new clothes for Europe and chose orange, the colour he wore at school. The T-shirt he bought was tangerine, with a red star across the front which carried the word 'Converse'. Next he bought a pair of red tracksuit bottoms, made from a thick elastic-type material, a black baseball cap to protect him from the sun, and finally a bag of cola nuts.

The streets of the Medina were largely unlit but residents had opened their doors hoping to stir the air and, in doing so, released pools of dim light into the evening, along with the smell of honey and lemon, chopped garlic and onions and sweet chilli paste which Justice felt catch the back of his throat as he walked by. In some places the streets were so narrow, it was like he wasn't outside at all but as if he were walking through a mediaeval kitchen busily preparing for some extravagant banquet. Justice considered returning to the shops for some bayrush but found he had no appetite.

He passed into a different zone where the doors were closed and the only light came from upstairs windows.

When he arrived at the post office it was quiet. There were three or four faces he recognised. One of them was a boy with yellow skin. Hong Kong they called him, even though he came from Togo. They were standing apart from one another, apparently there for entirely different reasons. On seeing Justice, one of them wandered away down a nearby street and returned a few minutes later. He looked up and down, and then set off again. The boy with the yellow skin was sitting on the wall. He nodded at Justice but stayed where he was. Justice positioned himself some way back from the street, in a shop front where he felt less exposed. It wouldn't be wise to be seen by the police hanging round the Medina at night.

Some time after nine o'clock, a car's headlights slipped across the T-junction at the top of the road and moved slowly towards them. It pulled up beside the post office, and the man inside whispered across to Justice, 'Lampa-lampa?' Justice climbed into the back and the others followed.

The vehicle was not what he'd expected. It was more like a taxi than a smuggler's car, with grey cloth seat-covers, the smell of stale tobacco and bright yellow prayer beads. The driver was Libyan. Justice never saw his face, only his eyes through the mirror, but he seemed middle-aged and drove along the unlit streets in silence. Justice was against the window on the driver's side with two others squashed alongside him in the back and one in the front. They sat, bags on laps, and watched as Tripoli, with Razak, Atiku and the rest, passed away behind them.

Zuwarah Beach lies about 70 miles west of the capital. The road from the Medina passes Gaddafi's compound, with its high security walls and prison-style watchtowers. Afterwards it narrows to a single carriageway, fringed with sand and wild cacti which spill over walls and stretch into the path of vehicles. There are technical colleges draped with Islamic slogans, single-storey homes protected by sheet-metal gates, abandoned diggers and concrete mixers. Down the centre is an aisle of orange soil from which sprout several kilometres of identical bottle-shaped palms.

'We change here,' said the driver in Arabic. He took a look in the mirror, switched off the headlights, and pulled sharply onto a patch of scrubland.

They were heading towards a dark shape which appeared to be the size of a house and was set some way back from the road. Justice knew they couldn't have reached Zuwarah, so the unexpected diversion caused him some concern. The route was rutted with tyre tracks and there were tufts of sand grass which scratched the underside of the car. They could see torchlight now and the driver was moving towards it. About a hundred metres from the road was a giant bush, its coarse dry branches thatched together into a desert nest. There was an opening on one side and the car drove straight in.

'Out!' They opened the doors and could taste cigarette smoke. Another Libyan was there, with a torch. He indicated for them to carry on walking, which they did, hugging their belongings to their chests. Deeper into the bush was a white pick-up truck. They were instructed to climb aboard and lie down, and then a blue tarpaulin sheet was drawn over them, 'like chickens,' thought Justice.

They felt the bump as the driver closed his door, then the chalk-board scraping of dry branches and the wheels drifting through soft sand. A short time later the driver moved up a gear, the tyres sounded sticky now and Justice assumed they were back on tarmac.

The next town along is Sabratha, where Roman remains tower from the sand. The shops sell tiles, cement and beach balls which hang outside in yellow plastic nets. Then there is the plain. The houses are gone except for sand-coloured igloos and wicker huts occupied by shepherds. To the left there are apricot-coloured dunes chiselled by the wind, to the right, a mile or so away, a cream thread divides the horizon. The men were close to the Mediterranean Sea. They heard the occasional car pass by in the opposite direction, but the road was largely quiet. The truck moved at a cautious speed and Justice guessed they were beyond the final town, on a stretch of road where the police often sat in wait. The time now would have been around eleven o'clock.

There are boat yards after that, two or three of them, selling wooden, open-topped vessels set out in single file by the road, leaning on their own keels. Many of them are painted sky blue on the inside and out. They're a similar shape and size to the ones you might use on a boating lake, with a couple of wooden slats for benches.

Soon, Justice became aware they were gliding across sand again. It was thicker this time and fizzed gently beneath the wheel arches. During the day, this is a flat, barren area with a sea breeze which paints the air orange. The surface is rutted with wheel marks, showing where people have come and gone from the sea. Every so often, there's an abandoned tractor or car, most of which have been set alight. There's little desert bush here and what there is can be used as cover for the Libyan border patrol vehicles, even at night.

After four hours on the road, the truck slowed and stopped. There were Arabic voices and someone began to draw back the tarpaulin. Justice and the other three stood behind a screen of bushes and dried fig trees. In front of them was a half-built house which occupied a dip in the sand where patchy grass had taken root. It was constructed from orange bricks, crudely glued together with crumbling orange cement. A couple of rooms had been completed but were still without a roof, and as for the rest, the builder appeared to have lost interest, leaving knee-high walls and rusting scaffold. Beside it was a tractor.

Justice could hear the sea, or at least what he guessed was the sea, although maybe it was the wind, or the beginnings of an electrical storm. The noise drifted in from the north, the only sound in the night, a distant velveteen rumble. Looking in the direction from where it came, there was not a single light, only blackness. Behind him, and some distance to the west, was the smooth outline of a mountainside, on top of which a red light flashed from a tall pole.

The room they were led into had a concrete floor and little else. There was no light other than that from the moon and Justice could see the outlines of several figures sitting with their backs against the walls. He and the others were instructed to move inside without a noise. The men in

139

charge were four young Libyans, who looked to be in their early thirties. One of them stood at the door to the room, smoking. Another indicated a place to sit. Then he demanded the money.

'Can we see the boat?' asked Justice.

'The big boat is far out at sea. You will sail from here in a small boat. That will come later. You must pay now.'

Those he'd travelled with were already rooting in their pants. However carefully he planned the crossing, it was always going to come to this. He would have to put his trust in the smugglers at some point.

Justice produced five hundred dollars and handed the money over. The Libyan smoothed the notes in his hand and tapped them together like a pack of cards. Then he lit a cigarette and joined his friend at the door.

Justice was in the last truckload. The others had begun arriving five days before. They'd been fed spaghetti and bread, and told they couldn't set sail until there were enough of them to fill the boat. They'd paid 1,500 dollars each. The price had dropped as the smugglers became desperate to fill the boat. The takings that night would have been around thirty thousand dollars. Remove the cost of the boat and the engine, and their human cargo was still earning them more in one night than an average Libyan would take home in a year.

'Hey, Justice . . .' The voice came from a man with his belongings stuffed in a plastic bag, and a Van Dutch hat pulled tightly over his ears. He rose to shake Justice by the hand. 'You never said you were doing lampa-lampa.'

'Neither did you,' replied Justice. He could see Atiku's face now, beaming at him through the dark.

'This is my friend,' shouted Atiku, 'we played football last week, and he didn't even tell me he was coming.'

'Shush,' said Justice, 'we are supposed to be quiet.'

Atiku lowered his voice to a whisper. 'Are you afraid?'

'I can't be afraid,' replied Justice. 'I have prayed hard for God to guide us to Europe.'

The smugglers provided cartons of milk, some biscuits and mineral water. Justice declined the biscuits. They were thin and anaemic, and anyway his stomach felt full, like there was food right up to his throat.

There were final preparations underway. Justice went into an anteroom and changed into the red tracksuit bottoms and orange T-shirt which he had packed into his Wayne Rooney sports bag. One of the Africans had brought a roll of sticky tape and was demonstrating how it could be used to make certain items waterproof. Justice removed the chip from his mobile phone, took a length of tape and wrapped it round and round, until the chip was sitting in its own plastic pouch. The phone he put in his holdall, the chip in his pocket.

The three Libyans were becoming increasingly anxious. One sipped from a bottle of spirits, the other two snatched at their cigarettes, blowing the smoke out like an irritant. At around three in the morning, the drinker left the room. They heard him start the tractor. The engine drifted away for a while and then returned at the far side of the house.

'Stand and follow.' They were led around the front, covering their faces against the loose sand. There was an outbuilding near to where the tractor stood. Its doors were thrown open. 'Go, go! Five of you go help. He needs help.'

Some minutes later, the Libyan with the bottle climbed onto the tractor and pulled it slowly away, revealing a small blue boat now attached behind. It was about the size of a rowing boat, with no visible engine, no seats, no life-jackets, no provisions – a decoy boat, that if spotted would appear to be nothing more than a fishing vessel on its way to catch the early tide. The men were instructed to put their belongings inside. They arranged them carefully on the floor, plastic bags tied with string, sports bags, jackets ready for a European winter, loose shoes. The boat smelt of fresh paint.

One of the smokers was in charge, 'These are the instructions: you follow the boat to the beach.' He took a tug from his cigarette, and flicked the stub away onto the sand. 'When I say "down" you get down. There is no talking.'

The driver of the tractor appeared quite drunk, smirking down at the men as they received the orders and occasionally shaking his head like a despairing schoolteacher.

'The weather is okay, the sea is smooth, the motor we have for you is the best,' continued the boss. 'So, you should not be afraid.' Beads of sweat had gathered across his nose and temples. As he spoke, he kept a hand thrust into his pocket like he was making a fist.

'Excuse me Sir, my name is Godwin, and I would like to say this: we have not been on a boat before so we need your help.'

'You will get our help. There will be water on board and food.'

'Thank you Sir, but some of us are worried about the boat. We haven't seen it yet.'

'The big boat is waiting for you, far out at sea. Trust us, and you will be fine,' the Libyan walked over to Godwin and leaned over him as he spoke. 'There is a smaller boat prepared for you on the beach and that will take you out to where the large metal boat is anchored.' He went back inside the half-built house and returned with an armful of baguettes, about twenty of them, which he dropped into the back of the boat. 'This will be enough for you but don't eat too much or you will become heavy and the boat will sink.'

At thirty, Godwin was older than most of the men at the half-built house. He had cheeks that were taut and round like chicken eggs, so that whatever his mood he appeared to be smiling. He disguised his height with a humbleness which seemed to weigh down his shoulders and make his body bow slightly at the waist. His movements were those of a man trying not to be seen. When he bent to pick up his belongings, he lifted them so gently from the ground into the boat, it was like his bag was covered with butterflies. Godwin had packed two shirts (both long-sleeved), one pair of brown plastic shoes, and some black trousers. He'd bought the trousers especially for the trip, folding them neatly to avoid creasing. Once he was in Europe, he'd wear them for job interviews.

'If you have anything metal with you, you must remove it now,' said the boss. 'Take everything from your pockets so we can see. If you take metal onboard it will affect the equipment.' He wandered round the group of men, examining the contents of their outstretched hands. 'Bank notes too, they contain metal.' Coins, rings, crucifixes, all were collected in a bag. 'Pull up your shirts.' Godwin revealed a narrow leather belt with a metal buckle. 'You must leave it here.' He unthreaded it, and dropped it inside with the rest of the things.

The tractor began to pull slowly away and the twenty-seven men tucked in behind it. The boss walked amongst them, whilst the other Libyan took up position at the front with a flashlight. The initial stretch was straightforward, they were protected by bushes and the Libyans seemed quite relaxed about the loose formation of the parade. But soon, the bushes gave way to open ground and the boss raised his hand for the men to stop. They looked around awkwardly, wondering what was to come next. Some removed their shoes and placed them inside the boat.

The tractor drew away again, but this time the men were ordered to stand still. They watched as it followed the tyre marks out onto the plain. The only light was the amber dot of a cigarette from the Libyan leading the way. After a minute or so, there were two flashes of the torch.

'Okay. Now, move like this,' the boss bent double and took off like a chicken.

The twenty-seven men followed and on reaching the boat tucked in behind him. For a time they appeared to be making good progress. The ground was a mixture of orange earth and stones, and the tractor rocked along quite easily. They used the boat for cover now, crouching on what they assumed was the seaward side. The taste of salt had reached them and Europe felt closer than ever.

Then there was a flash of the torch, the tractor jarred to a halt and the boss yanked the nearest African to the ground.

'Down. Now. Down.' Justice landed face down on stones by the side of the track, smooth flat stones. The tractor engine cut. There were no more instructions. If they were caught here, there was no cover, nowhere to hide. To his right was the red light on the pole. Up ahead, the tractor, and the decoy boat. All around, motionless bodies. The men remained that way for several minutes. Then, a torch flash, and they were on their feet again, scrambling along beside the boat.

At around 4 a.m. they came to a place where the sand turned soft and sloped gently away from them. Beyond, lay about a hundred metres of beach, then the still blackness of the Mediterranean. The tractor could go no further. The decoy boat was uncoupled and the men instructed to lift it and make their way to the water's edge. Justice had hoped to see lights from the metal boat. Atiku was more optimistic – he expected to find a container ship moored just off the beach. Right now, they couldn't even see the transfer boat.

It was when they arrived at the water that the first knife came out. They pushed the decoy boat across the beach and were instructed to carry on pushing until it was afloat. Justice wanted to retrieve his bag but the boss said all belongings should stay where they were. Then the Africans stood back from the water and watched as the Libyans pulled out an engine and struggled to fix it to the stern.

'Okay. You come here.' Nobody moved. 'You!' The boss shone his torch in someone's face. An African edged forwards, into the water. 'You pull this and the engine begins.' He used the beam to point out a rubber handle which dangled from the side of the motor by a cord.

145

The African turned and ran. One of the Libyans grabbed him. There was a skirmish. A knife came from his pocket.

'I will kill you,' he shouted. 'If you try that again I will kill you. Or we will call the police and let them deal with you.'

The drunken Libyan standing behind them on the sand also had a knife and began kicking up a racket. 'Police, police,' he waved his arms like he was rounding up cattle. 'Police, police. They will come if you try to escape. You must do this properly, or police, police.'

The men bunched around the stern, where the sea was at its most shallow. They couldn't operate the boat. No one had ever been near one before. There was supposed to be a captain. The drunkard was still shouting.

Then one of the Libyans was on board. He was scurrying around, manoeuvring large plastic containers, kicking their belongings towards the front. 'Quickly, quickly,' he seized hold of the nearest African and pulled him over the rim so his torso flopped into the boat.

The water was now above the waistband of Justice's track-suit. Those at the front reached out their arms to be pulled on board, scrambling over shoulders and heads. Once on board they crawled around, bumping into one another, trying to find a spot away from the water. They soon fell to the sides, legs tucked into their chests, knees almost meeting in the middle. The moment for escape had passed.

When around twenty had boarded, it appeared there was room for no more. But somehow the other seven squeezed in tight, right up to the bow where there was a covered space beneath which the bags lay. One of the men curled up inside it, away from the jostling. Justice was one of the last to board. His tracksuit bottoms hung from him like sodden towels and his feet slid around inside his trainers. He ended up at the rear, close to the engine on the right-hand side of the boat. Around his feet were several large plastic containers, each the size and shape of a suitcase. There was blue paint on his hands and knees.

The Libyan was perched on the edge of the boat next to him, feet planted on the inside, his rear hanging over the side. 'Okay, you pull this,' he tore a length of cord from the engine and it coughed into life.

'Is there no captain?' Godwin asked.

'I am the captain,' the Libyan responded. 'But if things go wrong you need to know how it works. It's easy.' He indicated some levers with the torchlight. 'Okay, so this . . . and then . . . move it . . . always . . .' No one was listening. 'Important . . . turn this . . . left, move it right . . . right, move it left.' Justice could see the phosphorescent glow of Zuwarah town, rising from the top of the beach to the south. To the east was Tripoli but it was far away now and the sky was black.

The Libyan ran the torchlight along a length of narrow blue tube, following it from the underside of the engine, into the nozzle of the nearest plastic container. 'This stays here . . . level of petrol . . . then change . . .'

Even though the man was carrying a knife, Justice was relieved he was coming. The other two stood watching from the beach. It was better the drunken one remained there. He was trouble and anyway they were out of room. Smoke rose from the sea around the engine. The Libyan was moving a lever which appeared to change the pitch, higher and higher until it fizzed like a drowning hornet. He pinched the blue pipe and stirred it around the nozzle. Then, gently, the boat began to pull away. Justice hardly noticed at first, he had to concentrate on the distance between himself and the shore to know it had moved at all. It cut smoothly through the water, the engine settling into a low hum and the Libyan now apparently content with the way it was running.

The mood onboard settled. It was a shuttle, a ferry service almost, which would take them to the waiting metal boat and then return to Zuwarah. The knives had been inexcusable but without them, it was possible some would have made a run for it. There were so many stories, how could they trust the Libyans? Both sides were taking a risk. The police had jailed people-smugglers before. No wonder there was so much tension. The Libyan knew they had to be off the beach before the sun came up, and when he returned alone, he'd simply be one of several fishing boats heading back towards shore for breakfast.

'When we reach the metal boat, the journey will be simple and next time you see the moon you will be in Europe,' the Libyan said. 'It's straight, straight all the way.'

He produced a large clock, with a dial and wide circular face. He laid it on his knee and tapped the side. Instead of a number 12 at the top was the letter N. He offered it to the men at the rear but Justice was more interested in the behaviour of the sea. It sluiced high along the side of the boat, no more than a couple of hand widths from the top edge. If he reached over he could touch it, which meant most of his body was beneath the water line.

They pointed at the stars and the receding coastline, and peered into the darkness over towards Tripoli. By now they were well west in a place where only fishing boats and smugglers sail. The breeze was calming and Justice leant his head back allowing it to cleanse away the tension of the last few hours. The smells of the land – the toasted fig trees, the charcoaled remains of cooking, the tobacco, the burnt sand, all had gone. Even though the wind seemed strong, the undulations in the water were long and gentle, not enough to break the surface. The boat itself was unworried by them, pushing along on an even keel so that they barely noticed its slow rise and fall. Occasionally there was an unfamiliar sensation, his body falling, his stomach remaining still. It was like he was being tickled on the inside.

'When you tire, you should help each other. No one should try to control the engine for too long. Remember, keep straight, straight all the way,' the Libyan pointed to the clock again and placed it somewhere on the floor in a bucket.

When he rose from his position, Justice thought he was going to deliver further instructions. He stood precariously close to the edge, with his hands away from the tiller. The boat seemed to continue in the same direction. The sea felt soft beneath them now, springy, like a car navigating through thick undergrowth. Then the Libyan turned away, lifted one foot onto the side of the boat and with a swing of both arms, launched himself, head first into the air.

Chapter Seven

The Libyan was in mid-flight. He was wearing a T-shirt and trousers, and yet he was heading for the water. The men hadn't had time to react. Some hadn't noticed he'd gone until the shouting began; they were looking ahead, or pointing at where the sky was just beginning to change colour to the east.

Godwin had his eyes closed and his chin resting on his chest, 'Thank you God for helping me find peace. I will tell my grandchildren how I came to Italy and they will praise you just like I have always praised you.'

Justice was sitting beside the empty space left by the Libyan. The jolt from his feet had dipped the rear of the boat beneath the surface so that a little water had streamed in on either side of the engine. The Libyan couldn't be jumping into the sea. It would be like leaping from a plane. The sea is no different from the air and only fish can stop themselves falling through, because they are light, like the birds. The boat can float because wood floats.

Justice couldn't swim. None of the men onboard could swim. Swimming was a gift, like being able to make leaves into medicine. Those who could swim must be able to render themselves weightless. You had to believe you could do it. It only worked for those who believed it. If you had any doubt and you threw yourself in then you would be punished for your doubt. Justice couldn't believe in it. His body was too heavy. He would fall right through and break himself on the bottom. Even his uncle had warned him against the water.

In Gurji, Razak was picking his way across the market square, through the cardboard boxes and piles of rotting fruit on his way to morning prayers. He wouldn't discover until later that Justice had gone. At the tin huts, the mattresses were scattered outside. When Justice failed to return last night, they finished the daggie and went to sleep. Now they could see his mattress was empty. 'Maybe he was kept late in the Medina. He'll be back,' they said. But they had been in Gurji long enough. They knew his mattress would still be empty when they returned from the workshops that night.

The two Libyans wandered back up the beach to restart the tractor. They would wait for their friend and then return to the half-built house where they'd drink a little more and sort through the bag containing rings, crucifixes and belts. The first time they did it, they may have been afraid the Africans would turn the boat around and come looking for them. Now they were not. They knew that once the men were out of their depth, they always behaved in the same way.

The twenty-seven were squeezed in shoulder to shoulder, trying to hide in the curves of the hull. The Libyan was in the air, arms and head pointing downwards into the white stripe stretching back to the beach. He was suspended for a moment and then he was lost in the wash.

No one moved. The engine continued. Then the man's head surfaced, they could see it against the white. He raised his arm from the water, held it in the air, and waved. The Libyan waved. It was a friendly wave, like he regretted having to leave; a sorry-I-have-to-bow-out kind of wave. And from the water he shouted. 'Keep straight. Keep straight and you will find Italy.'

Justice tried to scramble to his feet. Others did the same, but the boat rocked wildly, and they dropped back down. If there'd been a stone, Justice would have thrown it.

Godwin wanted to shout. He wanted to rage and cry and plead for God's mercy. But no one made a noise. The Libyan wanted them to die, he was certain of that, but if he bellowed his prayers across the sea, the wind might carry them back to the shore, up onto the road beyond the desert. What if the police heard? Even now, even this far out, they would still come for him. He looked at the faces. These were strangers, desperate strangers. If they thought he was going to give them away they might throw him overboard.

Then it began. 'You cannot leave us here, you are the captain! . . . We will die if you abandon us . . . None of us can swim!' The shouting was hesitant at first. Then they were howling and screaming like the Libyan was the last who'd hear them alive. 'You will go to Hell for what you are doing! You are killing us.' He kept on going, arms rising and dipping in the black water, whilst the boat took them in the opposite direction.

'Go after him. Turn it around.' They were wrestling now, on their knees, struggling to the front, but those who emerged breathless from the limbs and the luggage could only punch the water and make wild gestures as the Libyan vanished into the dark.

Not all were distraught. 'Let him go,' shrugged one. 'If he's gone, leave him. Many of my friends have made this journey. We don't need a captain.' The boy was smaller than the rest, wearing a green cotton T-shirt and jeans, like he was on a pleasure cruise.

Justice turned to him sharply. 'If you knew the conse-quences of what has just occurred, you would not say this. Do you know what happens to people out on the water?'

The boy looked away from the rest and said nothing. 'He must be a newcomer,' Justice said to Hong Kong. 'Anyone who's spent a season in Tripoli knows the dangers of lampa-lampa without a guide.'

The boat glided for a while and finally came to rest, engine idling in the water. Atiku reached out towards the metal bar, nudging it tentatively one way and then the other like it might be hot. 'If we don't need a captain,' shouted Justice to the boy in the lime green T-shirt, 'You come and make it go.'

'No,' he said. 'I won't do it. Someone else should start the machine.'

Atiku rested his hand on it, and then curled his fingers around the lever, twisting and pulling until the pitch of the engine changed and, very slowly, the boat began to pull away.

'We should go back!' someone shouted. 'If we return to

the beach we have lost our money but at least we have not lost our lives.' Others agreed. But none had any idea how to turn the boat around. The Libyan had never deviated from a straight line and now they were just following the course he'd set.

'Even if we knew how to return,' said Justice. 'We should not turn back. The Libyans would put us in an underground prison to live with the insects. We would be beaten, and there would be no one to hear our shouting. People would die there. It is certain.' Atiku tried twisting the handle a little further, and the engine's vibrations spread through the boat. 'There is no safety back there for anyone,' continued Justice. 'No peace. Why should we not continue? We have fuel and water. Some time tomorrow, when the sun is shining, we will see land and we will know our lives are beginning.'

All the men knew it. It was just instinct that made them lean backwards towards what was familiar; the dangling carcasses with their funny woollen hoods, the moonlit football and the camp fires upon which they poached soft goat brains in a bag.

As one of the last to board, Justice found himself at the stern, on the right hand side of the boat with just one person separating him from the engine. There was a narrow shelf around the inside of the craft about a foot from the floor, which the men were able to sit upon. Above it, the curved hull rose about another foot, and was finished with a topside rim which, when they leant backwards, reached about half-way up their spines.

There was little room for movement. The men were positioned facing each other along both sides, so that they formed a narrow gully down the middle between their knees.

Much of the fuel supply was packed around the area where Justice sat. It was stored in blue plastic tanks which were flat sided and propped against each other like giant books. They continued down the length of the boat, squeezed between the men's knees, along with the bread and the bottles of water. All their belongings were out of the way now, beneath the front, where they'd been kicked during the process of boarding. The boy who'd started the journey curled up beneath the hatch was now on top of it, one leg on either side of the bow, feet dangling just above the plume of water being ploughed at the front. 'The bravest man I've ever seen,' said Justice.

The rest of them were crammed down the sides, shoulder to shoulder, knee to knee, so tightly the boat itself could not be seen. On Justice's left, beside the engine, was the oldest man on the boat, a 42-year-old they called Uncle. On his right, the yellow skinned boy, Hong Kong. Opposite, and with his hand resting on the engine's metal bar was Atiku. At eighteen years old, Justice was the youngest on board.

He took charge of maintaining a steady supply of fuel to the engine. It was feeding from one of the tanks jammed between his knees, sucking the fuel along a narrow plastic tube. He would need to keep an eye on it, to make sure it didn't run dry. When the first tank was empty, they agreed he would remove the tube and quickly swap tanks, hopefully without stopping the engine in the process. In the meantime he held it firmly in place.

The engine itself was made of shiny blue plastic. There

was a metal leg which reached out of its base, down into the water. On its foot was something which looked like a ceiling fan, only smaller. On the casing was written the number '50' and the word 'Yamaha'. The metal lever with the black rubber handle protruded out of the casing and into the rear of the boat.

Thanks to his position beside the engine, and his willingness to take hold of it when the Libyan left, it was Atiku who found himself de facto captain. In addition to his trademark Van Dutch hat, he was wearing a cream sports jacket zipped at the front, a bronze coloured 'London-wear' shirt and baggy jeans, like someone was saving a place for him in a Soho bar.

It didn't take him long to discover that by twisting the rubber handle he could control the speed of the boat, but that if he tried to hurry her, the engine ploughed so deep and so hard that the rooster tail of water began sliding into the back. Atiku settled on the speed of a casual walk.

It wasn't arduous work, but the vibrations rattled his bones and blurred his vision. What he didn't realise was that the lever also controlled the boat's course. It didn't seem to matter; the white line they left was straight, and so he assumed they were heading in the right direction.

Further down the boat, at the point where its sides began to curve around to the bow, sat Godwin. Despite them being only minutes from Zuwarah, he was scrutinising the water ahead, looking for any sign of land. There was nothing, no lights, no earth breaking through, no branches. If he could walk on it, he would have climbed from the boat right there and then, and run on his toes as lightly as he could, so fast the fish couldn't catch him. He'd have been back on the beach in a matter of minutes, stamping on the ground, feeling its firmness and making promises to God never to go on the sea again.

He knew now, like the rest of them, that the Libyan had tricked them, that there was no big metal boat. But their course was set and they had no idea how to change it. So they pressed on through the dark hours of that morning, heading in the direction they assumed was Europe. There was little talking, and almost no movement. The boat was divided broadly into two sections. Those at the stern, who dealt with the engine, and the rest who, for the moment, just needed to keep still. If they could hold on until morning, they were confident they'd see the shores of Europe. To their rear, the street lights of Zuwarah town became indistinct, just a layered glow in the sky. The red beacon on the hillside was their last bearing. They watched as it fell lower on the horizon and finally dropped out of view.

That first morning broke calm with clear skies. The sun gently lifted some of the damp from their clothing, and warmed the men's spirits. Overnight they'd become more accustomed to their cramped surroundings and delicate stability, and imagined the most difficult part of the voyage completed. At least now they could see where they were heading.

'When we see birds we know land is near,' said Justice quietly. 'Birds need trees, and trees need land.'

He kept his voice low like they were passing through a forbidden place. He'd never seen such vastness, such lifelessness. At least in the desert you might find occasional scrub. There could be distant lights from Bedouins, or tyre tracks across the sand. Even at its most desolate you could see the work of the wind, the chiselled shapes in the sand, the cleanly sliced peaks, and you knew the wind had been blowing and that it would blow again, that there would always be change.

They'd been sailing now for some two or three hours and nothing had moved but the sun. Only the tapering white stripe behind them indicated they were making progress. But though the emptiness was disconcerting, at least there was nothing impeding their journey. The sea was quiet and it seemed God had come to visit. The job of searching the horizon was enthusiastically embraced by all, with the expectation land would be sighted before midday. Fifty miles, a hundred miles? It didn't matter. All that mattered was hours. That was the language of lampa-lampa.

From where he was sitting, Justice could see just how low the rear of the boat hung in the water, how close the sea was to the back edge. When the water was this calm, it wasn't much of a worry but every now and then it trickled over the back, usually from incautious use of the throttle, but sometimes as a result of a clumsy movement further down the boat. They were still discovering the limits of its stability. If someone attempted to swap places or merely adjusted their sitting position, the boat would tip to one side, others would instinctively try to correct it and the jolts would work their way along the boat until stability was finally re-established. The sea water formed a pool in the lowest part of the boat – the rear with its engine and heavy supply of fuel. Just before the Libyan left them, he'd placed the large clock in a bucket of sand, pressing it down so it stayed in position. Since they could find no purpose for it, they removed the clock, threw the sand overboard and used the bucket to scoop out the water.

Some time before noon one of the tanks of petrol began to run dry. Justice tilted it so that the green liquid collected in one corner, giving the tube an extra inch or so to work in. With his free hand he pulled a spare tank closer and unscrewed the cap. It had expanded in the heat and when the cap came away it gave a gasp beneath his hand. Atiku and the others looked on. Justice could taste the vapour in the air. He was ready for the first change. The remaining fuel barely covered the bottom of the tube. He waited a little longer, wondering whether he should pinch the tube between his fingers during the transfer, then whipped it out like a snake from its hole and plunged it into the next tank. He waited as he imagined the tiny air pocket working its way through. No one spoke. The monotone buzz was the only sound. Justice had petrol over his hands and fore-arms. He held the tube as still as he could in the fresh tank, trying not to disturb it any further, but there was nothing, not even a change in tone from the engine.

The boat had something like thirty tanks, or jerrycans, of petrol on board. Upon each was written '20 litres'. It's a standard size for that type of container. Taking into account the overloading, the size of the engine and the design of the boat, it's estimated that each container would have given them a range of little more than five miles. That's if the weather was calm. Five miles per can. That gave them an overall range of around 150 miles. The tiny

Italian island that Justice's boat was aiming at was 180 miles from where they left.

Either the smugglers thought the migrants would be spotted and rescued well before they reached land, or they were sending them to their death.

Towards the front of the boat, away from concerns about petrol and navigation, the mood was lighter. 'The sea is so big,' Godwin said, 'it looks like a giant football pitch. If I had a ball I could kick it higher and further than on the land. It would bounce on the waves like they were hills and it would carry on going.' His trousers were still coloured dark up to the waistband but the damp was warming. When he closed his eyes he imagined he was outside the Medina dozing on a wooden bench.

Beside Godwin was a 26-year-old Sudanese man called Daniel. He was smaller than the rest and spoke little; when he did so, it was in English. Daniel told them how his parents had been killed in the Second Sudanese War, a conflict which had claimed the lives of 1.9 million people. 'After they died,' he said, 'a group of men appeared at our home. "Here take this," they said. "Come and avenge your parents' death." And they offered me a gun.' Daniel didn't look at people when he spoke, but picked his fingernails or smoothed the creases from his trousers.

'What did you do with the gun?' someone asked.

'I didn't take it,' said Daniel. 'I left it with them. There was nothing for me in Sudan. Not one member of my family was still alive.' Daniel was one of four million people who've fled the country since fighting began.

'Why didn't you take the gun?' asked Godwin.

'I could not take a gun because of my religion,' replied Daniel. 'I am a Christian.'

Daniel described how he had travelled through the savannah of southern Chad, then north across the desert and into Libya. He heard there was work and stability, but ended up living rough, constantly fearful of arrest and detention. 'Even the police, they take the money out of your pockets,' he said, so he decided to move on again. Daniel said he saw on television that the streets in Britain were clean and that Africans looked relaxed and at peace. He heard they had jobs and families, that they were well treated. So, he decided to join them. It was Daniel who, when they were shouting at the Libyan swimming back to the beach, said they didn't need him, that they could make it alone. It was, as Justice had guessed, his first season in Libya.

On Godwin's left was a boy they called 'AK'. He told them how he was from a rural area of Ghana and that one day some locals had come to their house to circumcise his younger sister. She cried and protested, and that night, AK took her from her bed and the two escaped together across the border. They travelled north through Burkina Faso and then east into Niger. There they stayed in the capital, Niamey, for a while, but AK found no work. Eventually he left his sister in the hands of a woman who survived by selling street food. She agreed to help, on the condition he found a job and sent money back to them both. Now, several months later, they were still waiting. His crossing to Europe was on behalf of all three.

Godwin listened to each of their stories and then said they should all praise God and be grateful for this opportunity.

'We are all one now,' he said. 'If we work together like a family then that is the best way for us all to survive.' Then he filled his lungs with air and in a gentle, low voice, began to sing. As he did so, some of the other Ghanaians recognised the words and joined in.

> *'We will reach Canaan,*
> *No matter how arduous the journey*
> *We have faith that one day we will see the land.'*

It was a song Godwin learned at Sunday school, an inspirational song they would chant before playing football. Godwin was raised in Tema, the main sea port of Ghana. Every Sunday he walked with his parents to the local Pentecostal Church, a modern low-ceilinged building where purple velvet curtains hid the featureless walls. The congregation sat in rows on polished blond wood chairs, the women dressed in brightly-coloured hats, the men in suits if they had them. The preacher wore a white shirt buttoned right to the top, over which hung a chain carrying a large golden crucifix. The cross danced on his chest as he invoked the Holy Spirit to cure the lame and make the blind see. They called him a prophet and said that his faith was so strong, he could even make witches fall from the sky.

It was here Godwin studied the Bible and in particular the Old Testament. In a small annexe to the main church, he would sit on the floor with the other children and read verses out loud. 'To practise your English,' said the teacher, 'so that God will touch you with his grace.' They learned how Abraham's descendents fled a terrible famine by travelling south to where there was food. They went to a country he'd never heard of before, Egypt, but instead of being welcomed, they were enslaved. He imagined them in chains with metal balls attached to their ankles, working the fields to produce grain others would eat. Then he saw them escaping triumphantly, tens of thousands of them, struggling across hostile waters heading for Canaan, the place they could be free, Canaan, the Promised Land.

> *'I am thanking you, God, for everything*
> *You are my Lord and my Shepherd*
> *I am thanking you, God, for keeping me alive.'*

The songs kept coming. Some he'd learned. Others were fragments of psalms and prayers he'd weaved together into his own improvised hymns. On that first morning, it was Godwin's singing which set the tone for those at the front of the boat.

By noon, the sun was hanging directly above. Justice turned his black baseball cap around so that its peak protected the back of his neck. Further down the boat, Godwin removed his jumper and draped it over his head. There was no protection to be had on board, nowhere to find shade. Those without spare clothes to cover themselves, sat with their hands folded above their heads like schoolboys.

The food situation was another problem. Of the twenty loaves on board, many had become waterlogged by sunrise on the first day. Justice decided to treat this aspect of the crossing as he did any great test in his life. He fasted. It would help him keep a clear head and demonstrate his piety to God. Godwin decided to refrain from eating too, in case he put on weight and ended up sinking the boat.

It was some time during that first day that Atiku realised the metal bar could be used to change the direction of the boat. The discovery caused quite a stir. They noticed the white stripe in the water was no longer straight, but curved.

'You are taking us to our death,' someone shouted. 'Are you trying to kill us?' Atiku hurriedly adjusted the metal bar to bring it back in line.

The significance of the moment was not lost on Justice. 'Maybe we have travelled in a circle,' he said. 'Maybe we are heading back to Libya.' One of the men sitting near to the front was sick onto the floor of the boat.

The idea of not being able to see land hadn't really occurred to Justice. He didn't think the sea could be that wide. Even on the biggest ocean, land would always be visible as long as the sea was flat. If there were no hills on the water, and your eyes were good, the land would always be higher than the sea, so there should be buildings or mountains in the distance. But here there was nothing, only lines of smoke painted high across the sky. If he was up there with them, he'd be able to look down and see the world laid out like a map and tell the small boat which way to travel.

In the waiting room of Gurji, despite so many preparing for the crossing, Justice had never heard of anyone consulting a map. The last one he'd seen was the wall map at school, with the worn patch over Britain. Lampa-lampa was something the smugglers organised, the navigation was not the responsibility of the migrants.

Justice marked lunch with two swigs of water. The heat

and the dehydration were beginning to affect him. There'd still been no sign of land, yet the men at the front were constantly singing. He needed to speak to his God and the noise was distracting him. 'It's time to pray,' he shouted. 'My prayers don't match with the singing so everyone should pray, including the Christians.' Godwin and the others quietened down. 'There are twenty-seven of us,' said Justice. 'We don't know which one of us God will choose to answer. Maybe some of us are bad in our hearts and he will not hear them. But if we all pray, even if he answers just one, then the rest of us will also live.'

Justice reached behind him and dipped his hands into the sea. They felt mint cold like menthol where the petrol had splashed onto his skin. He rubbed them together and found a peculiar grittiness. When he'd washed, he reached back for more. This time he sucked a small amount from his palm into his mouth, swilled it around, and spat it back. The effect was overwhelming. It was like inhaling hot lemon. The sea burned the back of his throat and came up behind his nose making his eyes fill with water. But the ritual had to be done and better this than wasting drinking water. Next he dipped a forefinger into the water, raised it to his nose, sniffed sharply and cleared each nostril in turn. He did that three times as he always had. He cleaned his face with one hand three times, then his arms up to his elbows, then ran his fingers in a line from his forehead to the nape of his neck, just as he did five times every day. Atiku was going through the same process, as was Hong Kong and most of the other Muslims, carrying out their ablutions before what was to be an important prayer.

Justice dipped both his little fingers in the sea and ran them around the inside of his ears, following the grooves of flesh to the centre. Then it was time for his feet. He slid the whole of his body around trying not to disturb Hong Kong in the process and positioned himself so that he could clean them in the water. Then he stopped. What would they look like, these two wriggling black shapes, to anything watching from below? He decided against it, swivelled back round and washed them with sea water from the boat's floor.

Justice was disciplined about his prayers. He approached them with the determined concentration of the devotee, driving himself to another place where there was nothing other than his thoughts and the presence of God. There was a quote from the Koran he remembered loosely and which helped him reach the frame of mind he required. 'If you are worshipping me, know that I am in front of you. Worship me like you are seeing me, because I am seeing you.'

When Justice finished praying, his arms and face were white with dried salt. He looked down the boat and could see that all the other Muslims looked the same, white arms and faces as though they were painted and ready for war. The prayers seemed to have soothed the atmosphere, for a while at least.

'What will you do when we arrive?' asked Justice.

'I will be a fashion designer,' replied Atiku. 'Jeans and T-shirts, maybe shoes.'

'Inshallah. It will be hard work. You will have to study first.'

'I will study when I have the money. First I will do any job they give me but in the end that is what I will do.'

The others laughed with nervous excitement and allowed themselves to be spirited away to whatever was their vision of Europe.

'There will be big towers when we arrive, lots of them,' said Justice. 'People there live in high places, right up into the sky.'

'They eat burgers,' said someone else. 'McDonald's burgers and they're so round and neat they look like cakes.'

'There are so many jobs, everyone has one. Everyone. I have friends there, and they all have jobs.'

'They will give us the jobs they don't want.'

'Any work is good, anything.'

'Maybe I will help design the tall buildings,' said Justice. Others wanted to be engineers or cooks or mechanics.

'What about you, Godwin?'

Godwin looked smaller when he wasn't singing to God. 'When I was a boy, I wanted to be a politician,' he said. 'Like my father. That is what I wanted to be. But it is too dangerous. Instead I will buy a small bag of tools and I will do my house-wiring like I did in Libya,' he said. Godwin had his jumper tied around his head like a turban. 'My father will be proud, whatever job they give me. When I arrive I will tell people about the life of PW Akuamoah and what happened to him, and they will remember his story even though he never had the good fortune to visit Europe.' Some of the men had pulled their coats over themselves again for protection from the sun. 'I know that God is watching us,' continued Godwin. 'He won't allow us to die because I am the last of the line, the last to carry my father's name. If I die, everything comes to an end, so God will intervene.'

During that first afternoon, the non-appearance of land gradually silenced the boat. Uncle had been talking constantly in Justice's ear, recounting his life story over and over. 'I have a wife back home . . . there was a lot of crying when I left . . . the desert, I didn't even tell her about it . . . the children, I haven't seen them for two years . . .'

Justice couldn't bear it. 'I'm thinking,' he would say, or, 'I need to pray.' But Uncle's mouth carried on right into his ear. Even when he turned away, Uncle just continued, addressing himself to the back of Justice's head. He was trying to watch the white stripe. It was straight now, but how far had they travelled when it was curved?

'I need peace,' Justice finally snapped, surprising himself with the volume of his voice. Uncle nodded slowly, tucked his chin into his chest and began to doze. All they could hear was the slap slap of the water against the bow. The engine seemed softer now, like the wind which fluttered their makeshift turbans, and the gentle spray which soothed their cheeks. Silently swaying in the heat of the afternoon. Silently. Justice had drifted asleep and forgotten to switch to the fresh container of fuel. The engine had stopped. Atiku leaned over to shake his knee.

'What are you doing?' someone else shouted. 'Don't you care if we all die?' the man tried to stand, as if he were coming to sort out the fuel situation himself, but the rocking forced him down.

Justice saw what had happened and quickly transferred the tube into the next container. He pinched and wriggled it, and stirred it around but the engine remained silent. It was a strange sensation. They'd become accustomed to the constant buzz and throb. The machine was alive, and while it pushed them through the water it was their protector, their hope. Most of them had no idea what made it work. It could have required one can of fuel to keep it going for a year, or it could have run on milk, neither would have surprised them.

Without the reassuring hum, they realised for the first time just how isolated they were. The ocean was vast beyond what any of them had imagined. They couldn't understand how it could stretch over so much land and they began to wonder what lay beneath. When the machine was alive, it was a warning to anything living here that they were passing through, that they didn't want to cause any disturbance or to catch anything by surprise, like whistling to scare away the ghosts.

'How do you start it?' whispered a desperate voice. Atiku was jiggling a lever on the underside of the engine to no effect. He couldn't remember which bit the Libyan had torn out like a piece of string. The men were becoming agitated. They didn't want to be hanging around like this, attracting attention. Nothing seemed to have any give in it. The rubber handle which looked most likely was loose but Atiku only dared pull it gently in case it broke off.

For some of them this was a predicament only God could deal with. They bent their heads and began praying. Others squinted into the distance hoping to see a ship. Justice turned his body carefully so that he could peer down into the water, which he found was so close to him he could see his own face staring back. As he adjusted his focus, he saw they were sitting on layers of mirrors and glass suspended at different heights. Some seemed a long way off. Through them drifted an electric white dust, millions of particles which blazed and died in the refracted fingers of the sun. 'How deep is it?' shouted Godwin. Justice tried to keep his eyes fixed on one area, hoping the interlocking layers would at some point slide apart. 'It is maybe up to here,' he said, stretching his arm above his head. 'Too deep to stand.'

'You need to pull it like you're mad,' someone shouted. 'Pull it and the string will come.'

From a kneeling position, Atiku tried to rip the handle out of the engine. The sudden violent movement threw him off balance and set the boat lurching to one side. Some of them began scooping out the water. They'd all heard it though: something inside the engine had coughed. Atiku composed himself again. The men watched as he took hold of the rubber handle and in a flash threw his arm up and back behind his head. The engine coughed again, a whole series of coughs this time. Some caught and stretched out to reach the next, then caught again until they formed themselves into a line and sank into a low hum.

The men were overcome. They laughed and praised God and clapped their hands together as the boat drew slowly away. 'When we arrive in Italy I will give you my sister for marriage,' one of them shouted to Atiku.

The front of the boat had lifted slightly, allowing more sea water to spill over the back and they set to work with the bucket again. The sun was falling from the sky now and they needed to make haste. None of them wanted to spend another night out on the water.

Chapter Eight

'If there's a ghost alive in this world, they should guide me across the sea. If God is listening, please don't let me die, or all my father's enemies will laugh at me.' There was no right or left anymore. Another night had fallen without sight of land and Godwin was praying.

Cool air had moved in across the Mediterranean and a layer of mist had formed. Within it was a faint moonlight glow which seemed to be coming from somewhere beneath the surface rather than above. Where previously the night had been in sharp focus, now soft tissues of sea appeared to be drifting in the sky around them. The sound of the engine had changed, like someone had wrapped it in pillows.

Godwin was leaning forward, with his head in his hands and elbows resting on his knees. It was a position he'd adopted to allow the men on either side a little more space to breathe. They'd all been struggling to find a way to sit upright together. But when they did so, Godwin could feel their bodies expanding and contracting against his own and he knew they could feel the same. He'd tried taking smaller breaths so as not to annoy them and for a while even chose to lean his head and shoulders backwards out of the boat, with an arm looped around each of them, to give them room to breathe as deeply and as often as they liked. But his head had still been right up alongside theirs. They were sharing each other's air, sharing breath, out of their mouths and up his nose, and it felt hot from being inside their bodies, hot and rotten like they were digesting food in their lungs.

So, he'd lowered his head into the guts of the boat and found his face hovering over a rack of thighs, heavy sodden thighs and the smell of old sweat. Godwin tried to bury his head between his own legs. At least there, the smell was familiar. But he was still squeezed in so tightly he could feel the movement in his neighbour's muscles, the tightening of them when the boat swayed, the relief in them when it settled. He could feel the way their legs widened into their behinds and he knew that some time soon an acid warmth would seep from one side or the other and that he would say nothing.

With his head like this, he could press his knees against both ears and almost drown out the noise of the motor. It sounded further away now, detached from where he'd taken himself. His body moved with the motion, the rhythmic swaying, broken by the occasional jolt, but it was part of something else, something he'd left behind many years before. He remembered the muffled monotone of the engine as they raced through the dark fields, his face hidden, pressed hard against the car seat and sliding with each sharp corner, against the heat and the tears, squeezed in tightly alongside his father. There were four of them in all across the back seat. His father was leaning forward, over the arm rest, so he could shout instructions to the driver.

A few days earlier, Godwin had been in high spirits. It was the end of summer term and his mother had made the five hour bus journey to meet him at the Abetifi Presbyterian School, a fiercely religious boarding school situated in hills so tall that one missionary described them as, 'The Switzerland of West Africa, with nights as cool as May nights in Europe.' The school was a pink concrete building with staff bungalows and boarding blocks set amongst thick vegetation. Godwin thought the dormitory was more like a hospital than a boarding house, with grey linoleum floors, metal framed beds and matching cabinets each of which contained a single drawer where the boys were advised to keep their Bibles.

Even at fifteen Godwin welcomed his mother's bubbling displays of affection and the two of them chatted and laughed together as the bus drove them home, southwards through the fields of rice, yams and cocoa trees, back towards the coast and Tema.

Paulina Akuamoah was thirty-five years old and had a strong sense of right and wrong. If someone stole medicine from the hospital where she taught, or a doctor accepted bribes, she would remind them firmly but politely what the Bible said. Friends brought their children to her home for treatment and she would administer medicine, and even give injections. If neighbours fell on hard times she would take them food and money. Her benevolence had made her well-known in the area, but she wasn't sombre. Paulina Akuamoah could be dazzling, singing beautiful African melodies around the house, dancing to imagined tunes in the garden or at the market. It seemed God had blessed her with a vitality and generosity which she coiled around all she met.

The family home was a detached bungalow with four bedrooms, an indoor toilet and a broad tiled hallway containing a wardrobe, a chest of drawers and dozens of black and white photos, one of them showing his grandmother from the time when the British still ruled. White tiles, the floor had white tiles, he remembered that. That's where it happened. If it had been during term time, he might never have known. Not the detail of it, not the cracking sound in the evening air, the heavy boots or the sudden coldness behind the sitting room door.

The gang had run into the house and shouted so loudly. 'Where is he, where is your husband?' Godwin heard the commotion from the sitting room. He and the maid hurried into the hallway and saw his mother being confronted by four men. Three of them were dressed like government officials, plain black suits and white shirts. The other was wearing army fatigues, heavy black boots, a dark green beret, sunglasses. Godwin only caught sight of them for a moment but the military man was standing behind the rest, closer to the door. He was silent, taking in the family photographs hung around the walls, the paperwork stacked against the wardrobe, his father's jacket hanging from a peg. The framed picture of his father with the presidential candidate, Adu Boahen.

'Go back into the sitting room and lock the door,' Godwin's mother spoke calmly, as if she were asking him to bring tea and cake. The military man had a leather belt slung around his neck, taut over one shoulder. He looked at Godwin and then back towards his mother. 'Go back inside and I will be with you shortly,' his mother said.

Godwin and the maid followed his mother's instructions, gently closing the sitting room door. 'PW Akuamoah isn't at home at the moment,' they heard her say. 'Maybe you can leave a message for him.'

To Godwin's left was the sofa, where, until moments ago, he'd been listening to a quiz show on the radio. To his right was the dark wooden dining table around which his father held political meetings. The men in the hallway were becoming more agitated. Then there was a crack, like a firework in a can, and the shouting stopped.

Godwin sank down on the edge of the sofa trying to keep his breathing shallow, hoping he wouldn't be heard, trying to hide himself within. There was salt in his eyes. The radio was playing music now. He wasn't sure how long he and the maid had been there but his shirt had become cold and sticky. He heard boots tramp outside the sitting room door. They paused for a moment and then carried on down the wooden steps, through the garden where his mother grew vegetables, and out onto the road. An engine started and a car pulled away in the direction of town.

It was chilly in the hallway, just like it had been in the sitting room. The kitchen door was ajar. Outside he could see people and traffic. His mother was lying on the white tiles. She looked like a pile of clothes waiting to be washed. Some of the papers had been spilled onto the floor beside her.

Soon several party members were in the house. There was shouting. Cars came and went. Somebody was kneeling. His father appeared. Godwin was led into the sitting room. Hands stroked his head. A woman held his face against hers, trying to distract him. He was aware they were taking his mother. The voices moved from the hallway down the path towards the road.

The killers left a note folded on the kitchen table. It read, 'What happened here is just a warning. We will return again soon.'

Godwin watched his father going through the bedroom drawers. He worked quickly, sorting through papers, putting what he wanted into a bag. Files and a little money, everything else was left behind. He didn't even pack a change of clothes. Godwin had cried before of course, but they were the kind of tears easily distracted by a bag of sweets or a football. Now it was an illness, a sudden debilitating illness. The two of them hurried down the path to a waiting car.

It had sounded like they were arguing, like the men in the car were about to fight. He knew now they weren't, that they'd just been desperate, but he'd kept his face hidden, slipping against the leather and the tears. They'd been trying to find a place of safety then too, hurrying through the night with no idea where it would all end. 'What about Mr Kwabina, he supports the party, we could stay there for a while . . . No, it's the first place they will come looking, we should press on.' Along unlit roads, through strange villages, his father squashed up against him, restricting his breathing, still in the neat black suit he'd worn at the rally. Further away from home, swaying and slipping, and he knew they could never return, that he'd lost everything familiar.

In the early hours, they reached the home of his father's friend Adu Boahen, the presidential candidate for the liberal, property-owning, New Patriotic Party. The shooting of his mother and the long drive through the night happened in July 1992, just four months before the all-party elections, for which PW Akuamoah had been so actively campaigning and organising NPP rallies.

Godwin's father didn't want to intrude on the privacy of Adu Boahen. 'The gangs will have followed us,' he said. 'If we go inside, we will only bring Adu more trouble.' The other party workers insisted he should be taken there for his own safety but in the end PW Akuamoah and his son climbed from the car and caught a bus across the border into Togo.

And that's where Godwin and his father remained for the next seven years, living in hiding in the capital, Lomé. Presidential candidate Adu Boahen lost the election and even though the victor, Jerry Rawlings, swapped his military uniform for a suit, PW Akuamoah felt too intimidated to return to Ghana. Instead, he and Godwin lived like men on the run, no bank accounts, no paperwork, nothing to link them to the past. He took work as an electrician and never again involved himself in politics. He rented a kiosk, a wooden hut barely larger than a telephone box, from which he sold electrical wire, plugs and fuses. A discrete hand-to-mouth existence was, he felt, the most likely way to avoid the fate scrawled on that folded note.

In 2000, PW Akuamoah fell ill, but his refusal to seek medical attention left Godwin unsure as to the nature of his condition. He could no longer find the strength to open up the shop and instead sat listening to the radio all day whilst Godwin prepared food. After some months, he took to his bed and it was then he became anxious about the family name. If he died, he said, the ancestral line of the Akuamoah family would die with him. Not just him, but all those generations before him would have been defeated by a band of uneducated thugs who knew nothing of him but a name and address written on a piece of paper.

Before he died, he had a job to do. There were phone calls made and gatherings organised, and finally a distant cousin was located in Togo and invited to the house. The cousin brought with him his eighteen-year-old daughter, Rita. She had a pretty face, not dark black, but creamy, and Godwin thought her pretty, although he worried he didn't know what was in her heart. Some gin was found, Godwin and Rita stood in front of an audience of four, awkwardly holding hands, whilst his father read verses from the Bible. He ended by saying, 'You are now man and wife.' Then the toasts were made.

'Even if you must travel far to find work,' said his father, 'you should always send her money so that she can live happily. And one day, when you are ready, you must have children and you must tell them what happened to myself and to your mother so our names will not be lost.'

PW Akuamoah died shortly afterwards at the age of forty-eight. It was the second time in his life that Godwin properly cried. A few months after his death, in December 2000 the party he'd fought for, the NPP, finally took control in Ghana.

Godwin pulled his hood over himself to try to keep warm. There was some movement at the rear of the boat but he didn't look up. He heard voices and could tell they were in the process of swapping shifts. The boat slowed as someone took up position beside the engine and then pulled away again, gradually working its way back up to speed, with the same hum and rhythmic sway.

'You know I am in terrible difficulty and the sea might take us,' he whispered. 'But all I am is flesh and bone and I cannot do anything to influence the elements.' He was screwing his features tightly, willing her to hear him. 'You are closer to Him than me. He will hear my prayers through you.'

Godwin relaxed the muscles in his abdomen and felt the warmth spread around his thighs. 'I need you to plead to Him on my behalf,' he whispered to his mother. 'If you can see me now, see the danger I am in, please let us see lights, that is all I ask. We can take care of ourselves after that. But if we see no lights, there is no land. We cannot go on like this for long. The water and bread will soon be finished.'

Even now as he prayed, he could feel how taut his cheeks were against the crystallized salt. His parents' friends had always teased him for it. 'Look at that face,' they would say, playfully pinching his smile. 'Just like your mother – even if there's something to cry about, she will always find a better reason to laugh.' When he looked up, the shapes around him were blurred. The patch on his trousers had become cold and itchy.

Darkness felt like the most dangerous time. The mist lifted and the sky refocused. The texture of the sea changed. It seemed like water in a well, cold and lifeless, and at the edges it became one with the night. The jackets and jumpers they'd earlier used to protect themselves, had been dropped to the floor once the sun weakened and now they were heavy with water lying among the used petrol cans and sponges of bread. Most of the men were left in short-sleeved shirts and trousers. Not just one pair but two or even three. Removing their tops had been straightforward enough, but trousers, that wasn't even worth attempting.

Justice was on the tiller. It was his first shift and, as the youngest, he couldn't help feeling flattered they trusted him. He was determined to last longer than anyone else. The wind seemed to have picked up a little now. They were sailing straight into it and the skin on his arms had become like that of a plucked chicken. His tracksuit bottoms hadn't dried out during the day and hung heavily around his legs. That's what was making him shake, he thought, or maybe it was the vibration from the engine. His fingers, with which he gripped the throttle, felt like they'd shrunk inside the skin, and what was left was itching. Not the outside, the inside. When he tried to scratch, the itch turned hot and began to burn, despite his flesh being cold and numb.

Justice's feet were also causing problems. His training shoes had become tighter during the day and now they were digging into his skin. Either they were shrinking or his feet were growing. He wanted to reach down, separate out the toes and pat them back to life but they were squeezed between petrol cans with layers of limbs wedging them to the floor.

The rest of the boat was pretty much silent, apart from those mumbling prayers, or curses. Justice could see Godwin folded in two, with his head between his legs. Most of the others were upright, their arms across their chests. No one seemed interested in the horizon any more. At the bow, on top of the hatch, the silent boy had barely moved, his feet still dangling over the side.

Earlier, when Justice wanted to relieve himself, it had been a real rigmarole. He'd had to ask his neighbours, Uncle and Hong Kong, to push along so there was space for him to swivel round. Then he'd slid his knees beneath himself, turned his back to the boat, and tried to lean over so that none of it would come inside. But he'd leaned a little too far and had to grab Hong Kong's shoulders to stop himself tipping in. Then, when he was in position, he'd found he didn't want to go anyway. He'd never done it kneeling before, or with an audience, and his body just would not work. When he finally let it out, seated like the rest, he folded his arms over the darkening patch. He was downwind of them all, and was already being hit by waves of ammonia.

The sea had begun to change. Instead of moving smoothly across it, they were jarring against waves which ran in all directions. The movement was unfamiliar and the men gripped the bench. Empty water bottles slid from one side of the boat to the other. Justice was finding it difficult to concentrate. He couldn't get the story of Yunus out of his head. How would he spot a big fish in the dark? The water was on the move all around him, every swell looked like a black rubbery hump. How would he know the real thing? A jet of water. That's what would give it away, but in the dark, it wouldn't be easy. He'd shout them a warning, that's all he could do, but it'd be upon them in no time and then it was all down to God.

When Justice released the engine, he was still shaking. He said nothing, struggled across Uncle's knee, and left someone else in charge. It didn't matter who. And then he prayed and wasn't sure if he was saying the words quietly or out loud to the rest of the boat.

Godwin hadn't stopped praying. 'If I get to Europe, I will make money and one day I will return to your grave and I will lay flowers there, and I will sit with you and I will tell you all about my new life.' It was more like a conversation now. He was talking to her and he knew she was listening. She'd stepped right in from the sea and merged into him, like in the Bible, he was filled with her spirit, and only his body was having to contend with all this, only his shell. He and his mother were together and warm. The waves might shake the boat and turn it over but it wouldn't change a thing. 'And you will know that all the good things that have happened to me are because of you, and you will know that you can carry on living through me . . .'

Some time on that first night, a shout went up. Justice felt his muscles tense. One of the men had seen something in the water. The boat rocked with anticipation. He was pointing far to one side. It could have been in the sky. Justice could see it now, a floating light, several of them, in fact, a tightly packed constellation of red and sharp white. It's a wonder he hadn't noticed it before.

'It may be a house or a tower,' someone shouted. 'But whatever, we should go there. Something alive has made that light and around it we will find people.'

'It's not land,' said Atiku. 'It's a ship. I watched them at night from the benches at the Medina. They're giant things. If we go there, they'll have room for us.'

'What happens if it is heading back to Libya?' said Justice. 'We get there and they wave us on board, and then we discover they are wicked people trying to trick us?'

'It's better than dying,' said someone else.

'It's the same as dying,' replied Justice.

It was agreed the lights couldn't be ignored. If they discovered it was a ship heading for Libya, then they would need another plan, but for the moment, the salt-glazed figure of Atiku set a new course and in his eagerness, he over-twisted the throttle. This time they needed water bottles as well as the bucket to bail themselves out.

When the waves passed beneath them, the boat was so overloaded there was a pause before it responded and each time it ploughed deeper before righting itself. The wind occasionally caught the top of a wave and tipped it over the side. Several of the men were now working to keep the water out, mopping it up with clothing and wringing it over the side. Justice was sure there was a leak. There had to be. There was more water inside than he'd seen coming over the edge.

'*When Yunus ran away, like a slave from captivity, into a heavily laden ship . . .*' They were the words he'd read at school. He'd imagined them in a wooden boat, sea raging white around them, their cries thrown to the wind, water sweeping across the deck. '*The Lord sent a great wind into the sea, and there was a mighty tempest in the sea, so that the ship was likely to be broken . . .'* It was always dark, and they were kneeling in a circle, looking to heaven and praying to God. But now Justice realised that at the time, he'd only played the scene out in two dimensions. There'd been no down. They may as well have been on dry land. They were fragile only within the limits of his own experience. He'd never considered the great depth from which the big fish had come and into which they might sink.

'More lights!' someone shouted. And there were, far away, blinking just on the edge of things.

'The first is better,' said Justice. 'It was what God offered when we were praying hard.' And they pressed ahead, following the light at the bottom of the sky.

'All we need to do is get close,' said Godwin. 'The men on board will see us and they will come towards us.' He dropped his body forward again so that only his back was exposed to the wind. Over his head he pulled a green parka jacket, soaked and smudged with blue paint from when they'd first boarded. It covered almost all of him. The air inside warmed up quickly but he was left fighting for breath so he opened a flap and allowed the outside air to leak in. Now he could concentrate again.

After an hour or so, there'd been little progress, and the men were becoming uneasy. If anyone tried to move, there was shouting and some had even been wrestled back to their seats. The waves, too, had worsened and there was talk of throwing things overboard. 'Some of the bags, we don't need,' said a voice. '. . . and the petrol weighs too much.'

'The petrol should stay,' said Justice. 'You can throw my bag over. I have everything I need.'

'No, not a bag,' said someone else. 'It's too light. We need something bigger.'

Godwin kept his head buried between his knees. He'd read the story at school as well. '*Then the mariners were afraid and cried every man unto his God and cast forth the wares that were in the ship into the sea to lighten it.*' The mariners' boat had been sinking because God was angry, not with all of them, just with one. He remembered now; all the mariners got together and drew lots and whoever lost was the one who they should blame for being the cause of the storm. And one man did lose. '*And he said to them, take me up and cast me forth into the sea, so shall the sea be calm unto you, for I know that for my sake the great tempest is upon you.*'

Maybe there was someone like that on board now. It wasn't him, he was sure. It was someone with an evil spirit and whoever it was, they were putting everyone at risk. That quiet boy at the front, the one astride the bow, he'd taken no food or water yet. When the waves broke across the front, he remained still. Who knows, the water had probably even touched his feet, but he remained still as a carving. Why hadn't the waves taken him? He was wearing just that lime green T-shirt, but Godwin could see no shivering. He'd not complained once, even when the rest of them were trying to hide from the cold, and Godwin hadn't seen him pray. They couldn't afford to have one drop of evil onboard, things were too finely balanced. If he was a witch something had to be done.

There were others though. He'd heard some of them

whispering about money. There should be no money on board. The Libyans told them to put it in the bag. Maybe someone had been disobedient and kept something they shouldn't. If they were hiding money in their pockets they'd broken the rules, they'd deceived the Libyans. It was dishonest and now look. The sea was boiling and they were so ignorant they didn't know what they'd done. If they had any money they should throw it away, that way they could all find some peace.

And what happened to the man who'd drawn the lot and had been pitched into the sea? God had still looked after him because he repented. And he'd sent the big fish to eat him. Three days and three nights he'd been inside the thing. Godwin imagined the man kneeling in a dark cave, shaking with fear and whispering words of such piety and grace that they took him right up alongside God, so that he spoke to Him directly and actually heard His voice coming back. And he wondered why he hadn't repented when he was still on the boat and why God had risked everyone else's life because of this one man's disobedience. It was the same story Justice had read, only the name was different. In the Koran the man was called Yunus, in the Bible, Jonah.

The lights appeared to be on the move, drifting slightly to their left, and the men followed. It was approaching dawn when the engine calmed to neutral and the boat patted to a halt. Godwin looked up. Not a man was moving. He thought they were all asleep. How could they be when his brain was so hot? Then he realised they were praying, every one of them, apart from the quiet boy on the hatch, and Atiku who was slumped beside the engine.

So far, the job of handling the tiller had fallen only to the men at the back but this time none of them moved. The journey to the engine wasn't straightforward. Godwin put his hands on the bench either side of him and lowered his rear gently onto the floor. The water there smelt of petrol and urine and soaked quickly through his layers of clothing. He was on his back now, wriggling along propelled by his elbows, through the narrow gap between their knees. For a moment it felt safer lying in a shallow hole looking up at their faces but he carried on towards the stern, negotiating fuel tanks and feet, trying to keep his body in line with the boat's spine.

Some of the men took exception to the disturbance. 'What are you doing?' shouted one. 'Are you trying to knock us overboard so you survive and we don't?' Godwin apologised and moved on, until his feet were beneath the engine. There wasn't even room back here to put his hands on the bench, so he grabbed whoever's legs were on either side and levered himself into position.

Atiku had changed. His hands were wrinkled like an old woman's. Beneath his nose were snail smears which ran down over his lips and continued to the bottom of his chin. His face wasn't just pale with salt, it seemed like the blood had been drained out of him, leaving a yellow rind, like the skin on the soles of his feet. His eyes were red and raw like he'd been crying. The hat had gone and his hair had become crusted like it was sprinkled with sugar. His sports jacket hung low and lifeless, and inside Godwin could see that his body was trembling.

It occurred to him that the small circle of men who'd

been prepared to steer all had similarities in their lives. They were the ones who'd suffered the most, who'd looked into the heart of things and preferred this darkness to what they'd seen in others. At least if it was going to happen here, there would be no sharp edges, no broken bones, only soft water to take them home. Godwin took the tiller and felt the vibration spread through his body.

When the sun rose on the second morning it brought less clarity. The boat which had stood out so sharply against the night sky was now indistinct amongst the numerous white caps covering the surface.

'Perhaps it's sailing far away,' said Justice. 'There'll be food and water on board. Plenty of it. Enough to keep the passengers alive for several days.'

'So, they can share it with us,' said Uncle.

'I'm saying they're in no hurry. Maybe they are travelling to another sea not to land at all, like a holiday or something. How do we know? Only God knows.'

'God wouldn't let us follow the ship if it meant we would all die,' said Godwin.

Justice thought about it. He could see the temptation of following the boat, but it was like leaping from a high mountain or the pinnacle of a temple and expecting to be caught by angels.

'We should stick to what we know, not what we hope,' said Justice. 'Let the big ship go. We should change our course.'

'But this is what we know,' protested another man. 'The ship is going to Europe. Remember when we first saw it, Libya was behind us. That is for sure. The big ship was going straight, so it must have been heading for Italy.'

'How do we know we were going straight at the start?' asked someone else. 'Maybe Europe was behind us when we spotted it and the boat was heading for Libya.'

Justice had to stop himself shouting. If he'd been in the desert, he would have shaken their hands, wished them luck, and headed across the dunes alone in the direction of his choice. If later it turned out he was wrong, then so be it, he would die from his own mistake, not someone else's. But here, there was no escape, everyone had to conform to the majority view, even if they considered it plainly flawed.

'Listen. The only certainty is that the sun will rise. And the place in which it rises has always been the same.' He felt so much stronger on his own. Some of these men would follow the ship to the last drop of petrol and then pray for God to lower the level of the sea. 'When I pray,' he continued, 'I pray to Mecca. That is what all Muslims have been taught. We know that Mecca is where the sun rises and we know that is in the east.' Some of the men were whispering among themselves and gesturing towards the ship. 'So, if we know that Mecca is east, then we must keep it to our right, and we will be travelling north. But look where it is, it is behind us. We are not travelling in the right direction at all.'

'But we don't know that Europe is north any more,' said someone else. 'We are lost so maybe it is now to our east or our west. That is just as likely as it being north. Only the ship knows for sure, only the ship.'

Several others agreed, and Justice decided to wait. Some would become weaker during the day and then their ears would open.

The threads of smoke across the sky no longer had a visible source. The planes must be high, thought Justice, almost on the edge of space. If there was an airport nearby, then they would fly lower. He'd seen them passing over his home town heading for Accra, always on the same line, always at the same height. He used to think there were roads up there, invisible roads, maybe constructed from glass, a whole network of them across the sky and that planes didn't actually fly, they just drove along them until they needed to get off. But when they were this far away it was not a good sign. It meant they were far from land.

The sun touched its highest point and the men were quiet again. Several had wrapped themselves in damp clothes and chose to shiver rather than take the full force of its rays. The white caps were forcing the engine to work harder and some skill was required now to navigate. When a wave hit the front, or rose behind the engine, it deposited much of itself inside, and so they were forced to slalom through the water. The hurriedly constructed fibreglass shell was now being tested.

It was whilst Justice was making his ablutions that he saw it for the first time and snatched his hand away from the water. It was like a bird had crossed the sun, or a cloud had cast its shadow, but there were no birds and the sky was empty blue. It had slid by without causing a ripple, dark and featureless, and larger than the boat. He had a sense of its speed but not of its means of propulsion. The shape didn't linger, it was dynamic and purposeful. He shouted to the others and braced himself for the bump.

'Oh Jesus!' shouted Daniel. He fell to the floor with his face in his hands. 'Oh Jesus!'

'You said we should let the Libyan go,' Justice shouted down the boat. 'I told you people are dying in the sea. Now look. Go on, look. This is what we have now.'

Daniel was on all fours, his head hanging in front of him and his whole body trembling. Justice peered over the side. There it was again, like a swarm of locusts, flying in formation just a few feet beneath. It changed direction and flashed silver in the sun.

'It's gone,' said Justice.

'What does the sea look like?' Daniel shouted. 'Is the sea going to take us?'

'You should look yourself. Are you afraid now, the boy who set off with so much courage?'

'Oh Jesus!' Daniel cried again, his head buried on the floor.

Another man was leaning backwards and talking to the sky. 'Father in the mighty name of Jesus,' he shouted. His arms were raised above his head with his palms facing upwards. Sometimes his mouth would carry on moving, but instead of words, only sounds emerged. The man was speaking in tongues.

Daniel was crying without shame, great sobs and then, 'Oh Jesus, Oh Jesus.' His trousers had dark stains around the front and back. 'Oh Jesus, please do not let this happen, please deliver us from this evil.'

Now some of the men decided to resurrect the compass, placing it on top of a pile of clothes and trying to prod it into action. One man claimed to know how it worked and was shouting above the others that they should follow the needle. Someone else wanted everyone to check their pockets to make sure no one was carrying metal. 'It should have been put in the bag,' he said, over and over again. Libyan bank notes were produced from somewhere and thrown into the wind. 'Paperwork too,' shouted someone else. 'There should be no paperwork to link us with Libya.' More items were tossed overboard – mobile phones and notebooks. 'Keep your money,' someone else shouted. 'In case we need to bribe an official.'

Godwin could not believe what he was seeing. All this disobedience. Why had they kept the money? Didn't they know it could bring calamity? Now it was floating in the water around them, and there was more, the men were pulling it from their underwear, soggy grey handfuls of it.

'And food,' someone shouted. 'Any food they didn't give us. They told us not to bring food.'

One man had a packet of biscuits. They were in a bag around his feet. 'Throw them,' his neighbour said.

'But we could be on the sea for days.'

'Not if you throw them,' and with that, he dipped into the bag, and threw them over the side.

'Listen,' shouted Justice. 'We know there is land between here and Mecca. It may be several days away but we know the sea must end before we reach there. We should follow the sun.'

'But the finger is pointing us north,' said the man with the compass.

'We don't know how it works. No one does. It could be telling us to return to Libya.'

'The only humans near to us are on that ship,' shouted

someone else. 'If we keep following we might still catch it.'

Godwin's father had taught him to enter a debate only if he had something new to offer, and now he felt he did. 'Any land would make me happy,' he said. 'Any land but Libya.' They all agreed, and Godwin continued. 'I had some friends doing lampa-lampa last season. There were about thirty of them on the boat and they were all very much afraid. After some days they realised they were lost in the middle of the sea and didn't know whether Libya was behind them or in front.' The men listened quietly. 'Seven days passed, they had very little fuel remaining and some of the men felt they might be close to death. Then they saw a boat approaching. It was a speeding boat with people on the deck, and they knew that their prayers had been answered. But when it came closer, they realised it was not what they thought.'

The men had heard about patrol boats in the Mediterranean. They knew what they were doing was illegal but that if they were picked up outside African waters the attitude towards them would change. It was said European patrols would lift you from the water and take you to safety. You would be given food and medical attention and then you'd meet officials who would decide whether or not to allow you to stay. Even if they said no, many migrants phoned friends in Tripoli to say they'd stayed anyway and were looking for work on the black market.

There was another place they'd heard would send out patrols – an island near Italy. Like the others, they wouldn't turn you away and they would rescue you. But they'd sail you back to their island and put you in metal cages like murderers or tigers. The island obviously had to be avoided, but the men in the boat didn't know where it was, or what it was called. Then there were the patrols from Africa. It was said if the Tunisians caught you, they would take you to land, drive you back across the Libyan border, dump you if you were lucky, and hand you over to the police if you weren't. It was the Libyan patrols which were the ones to be avoided.

Godwin continued, 'So the men saw the writing on the side of the boat and they knew it was the Libyan police. Some of them were stronger than the rest. They told the others they didn't want any more problems in their lives, that they were tired and that they'd made a decision. Rather than return to Libya, they threw themselves into the water, eight of them, and drowned themselves right in front of the rest. Even the police were shocked. They took the others back to Libya and instead of throwing them in jail, they told them to go home and rest. I am telling you now, if the Libyans come to us, I will do the same. I will not even think about it.'

The others nodded. Several said they would do the same.

'So, whichever direction we choose,' said Godwin, 'it must be the one least likely to end in Libya.'

Atiku pushed the tiller away from him. 'Further,' shouted Justice, pointing in the direction he thought the sun had risen and the boat was turned fully around. They watched the big ship blink once or twice to their rear and then they were alone again.

Over the coming hours, it was difficult to determine progress. The water slid beneath them so that it seemed they were moving backwards. It drew itself into steep banks, higher than the boat itself until they feared the waves would smash down among them. The wind lifted spray from the sea until there was not a dry thing on the boat. And still the quiet boy sat atop the hatch.

Justice surveyed the slumped bodies. Who would be first, he thought. Whoever it was, the rest would expect him to deal with it. He was the youngest but he seemed to be the bravest. He hadn't cried yet. He couldn't just leave a body amongst them. He thought of the workshops and the hanging goats and the smell when the sun turned flesh green. But neither could he bundle it into the water. 'Don't look into their eyes,' he told himself. 'Otherwise when they die you will see those same eyes again, and maybe they can still see you even though their heart has stopped, and their spirit will follow you even if you survive and it will keep on following you to the grave.'

The water was slipping over the back faster than they could bail it out. 'There must be a hole,' Justice shouted above the wind. Some of the men had begun scooping with their shoes.

Justice opened his eyes and it was dark, closed them and it was light. The petrol tube slipped from his fingers. The engine died and then began again. The sun shone cold and the moon dried him. And then, on the afternoon of 25 May 2007, they saw something in the water – a structure. It seemed to be fixed to the spot. How far away it was, they could not tell. A fresh course was set and just before sunset they were close enough to see what they had found.

Chapter Nine

'I can see people,' shouted Justice.

The engine was digging low, water pouring over the stern. So much water. Atiku was pushing it hard and the cold was mixing with the warm until the water was up around their calves. White crests visited from all directions, so that the surface was all suds. They leant forward, away from the deepest water, but it was up inside the hatch now, dragging out the bags and spilling the contents down the length of the boat. It didn't matter any more. They were almost there.

Ahead of them, no more than two football pitches away, was a large metal boat; an arc perched high on the water. It was five, maybe six storeys high with sheer sides from which the waves fell backwards like they were rolling from a harbour wall. At one end of the deck was a white metal tower attached to which were all kinds of masts and rotating arms.

They could see them now, four men, leaning against a fence on top, smoking and staring out to sea.

'Please save us,' shouted the migrants. 'Our boat is broken.' And they waved their jackets in the air and bellowed so loudly they thought that even God must hear.

The men on the metal boat stood still, thick arms folded and patterned with tattoos. 'Europeans,' Justice said. 'Italy or Spain,' and he'd never given up hope, not once. In all this emptiness God had provided this single strip of solid ground where there should be none and He'd guided them to it.

'Save our souls,' screamed Godwin. 'Save our souls.'

The migrants were so close they could see the unevenness of the treacle paint and the bronze stains where the chains disappeared into its side. There were metal wheels with teeth, thick grey ropes, hooks, handles and oily sheets. It was a factory, a barnacled factory, creaking against the force of the sea. And it was a beautiful sight.

From high above came a voice. They struggled to catch the words at first over the wind and the sound of the engine.

'What do you want?' it said.

One of the Europeans was leaning over the rail. He wore only shorts and a golden necklace, his stomach was pressed out tight, tanned and round. In his hand was what appeared to be a gun.

'We want to come up,' shouted Justice. 'Our boat is full of water. Please, we need to hurry.'

The man nodded and turned away to talk with the others. Then he was back at the rail.

'Where are you going?' he shouted.

'Europe. Anywhere in Europe. We need help.'

'Well there's no point in coming up here,' the man replied. 'You're nearly there.' Then he gestured behind him. 'Just continue in that direction, straight, straight all the way. In two hours you'll be in Italy.'

'No,' went up the shout. Some held out the palms of their hands. 'We are too many in this boat, we cannot go any further,' they pleaded. 'The sea will take us.'

'If you keep a good speed, you will arrive before dark.'

'We will die.'

'There's not enough room for you and anyway we're staying at sea for days.'

Justice was looking for stairs or a window, anything to grab hold of.

'We will eat little. Put us all in one room. We won't interfere with your work.'

'There is no room here,' the voice said again. 'You must carry on. I will phone people and tell them to expect you.'

All of them began shouting at once. Atiku twisted the throttle and swung the boat round so that it was facing the metal wall. He paused for a moment and then accelerated. They were ten boat lengths away and heading straight for it. The water slewed up the sides and emerged from the back, hot and smoking.

'Why didn't you save us? screamed Godwin. 'You were our salvation.'

Three boat lengths away. As quick as the engine would carry them. The silent boy defiant on the hatch, poised as still as a figurehead. Uncle trying to wrestle Atiku's hand from the engine. 'No, please no,' he was crying. 'We will all be dead.'

The impact, when it came, was less violent than Justice had anticipated. They were jolted forward, some slipped from the benches, but there was no smashing sound, no splintering. Instead there was a woody thud, like two heads hitting, and the boat skewed to one side.

As it did, they caught the cap of a wave and were raised about a metre or so up the ship's side. Silent boy grabbed something. It was a rope or a tie. He was on his feet, pirouetting for a moment on the hatch. Then the wave fell away, drawing the boat back down, and leaving him dangling, hands above his head, feet scrambling against the metal as he tried to find some purchase.

They scraped down the ship's side, water yawning until they were against lime green. Out of reach above them was silent boy, twisting on the end of the rope. Then the swell lifted them and pushed them wide. Atiku circled back round and as they drew alongside, Justice planted his palms against the cold metal to try to steady them. It felt like tree bark after rain and he padded hand over hand until silent boy was directly above. A wave lifted them, spurting up the gap between the two boats. Their hands reached out, so many they were sure he'd be safe, but silent boy was strong and seemed to prefer the dangling rope. Next time, they made sure and yanked him back into the doomed vessel alongside the rest of them.

The white men had been watching. 'Stop what you are doing,' one shouted through cupped hands. 'Do not try to board the boat.' They were no longer smoking. One was on the phone, gesticulating and running his hand back and forth over his head. 'If you try again, we will shoot you.'

'Down, down,' Godwin whispered. 'We must all stay quiet.' They sat uneasily in the water for a while.

The conversation on the phone ended and it seemed a decision had been made. 'Okay, you need to go around the back. When you get there you will find some ropes that lead away from the boat. Follow them. Don't hang on to them, just follow them. When you get to the other end there is a place for you.'

At the back were two giant metal arms reaching out from either side of the ship to form a high arch over the stern. A small wheel hung from its centre and a single rope stretched away, taut as if it was dragging something heavy. At some point the rope divided into five, fanning out towards what appeared to be a fence in the middle of the ocean.

The migrants left the lee of the metal boat and headed straight for it. As they drew closer they saw the fence was fixed to a black plastic pipe which surged above the surface for a moment and then sank back down, leaving only the fence jutting above the waves. As the sea changed shape, the pipe reared back again, sleek, shining and serpentine. There was still a stretch of open sea to go and the men were pressing to the front, wrestling for the best position.

'Sit! You will tip the boat,' Justice was still at the rear. Others were kneeling to face the water, jackets hanging over the edge, preparing to grab the pipe first. Justice didn't think the fence would take their weight, not all of them. It was barely afloat now. There were balloons strapped around it, inflated plastic balls, but they were struggling to keep it from sinking. It would support a couple of men, maybe, but not twenty-seven?

'Sit . . .'

'No, you sit . . . You're trying to kill me so that you can be saved . . . We will all die if you don't sit.'

Silent boy had managed to slip back onto the hatch, he was going to make it first. Justice had too many bodies to scramble through, unless the boat came in sideways. Atiku was trying to see over the bobbing heads. He steered the boat in an arc. It was the left-hand side that was going to touch first, not the front. The left-hand side, Atiku's side. Only one or two to scramble through. But they'd noticed – the right-hand side had noticed and they were up and off their seats, clambering to the left.

'Back, get back, we will tip.'

But there were too many of them, prising and pulling. Some were torn from where they'd been sitting and thrown to the back, clothing ripped, limbs trodden. They were roaring with life, snarling and riotous. It was all in this moment now, the pack dripping and breathless. It all began or ended here. Then the boat wheeled gently over and slipped beneath the waves.

The shock of entry snapped Justice's lungs full of air and then he was under the water. Silent. Dark. Beneath him the sky. He punched and kicked. He sensed the water in motion, the swell breathing him in and then out. And he was suspended there for a time, in a place from where he'd once come. At last his head burst free, and he was back, back in the light and the din, fighting for tight little breaths.

There was a rope, a thin plasticised piece of twine. Justice grabbed it and pulled, but it was limp. He pulled again, passing it through each fist, then out and behind him.

Finally it jammed tight. He was lying horizontal, hands clasping the rope, legs splayed froglike. In this position he was able to pull himself slowly towards the black pipe.

The shouting was muffled, distorted, like it was from inside a bottle. Names, prayers, instructions. Some had made it onto the pipe – fifteen, perhaps twenty of them. They were hauling others from the waves, balancing precariously, water swilling over their feet. Another one, and another, and still it took their weight.

Justice was one of the last. They pulled on his rope and reeled him in like a fish. He knelt on all fours, breathless and spitting. '*In the name of Allah, the compassionate, the Merciful . . .*' The pipe felt smooth and hard, not metal, but plastic, thick and strong. '. . . *When the sky is rent asunder, when the stars scatter and the oceans roll together, when the graves are hurled about.*' If they were going to die it would have happened already, the boat had been taken away but He'd created this, a fence on a pipe, and dropped it right into their path. '. . . *each soul shall know what it has done and what it has failed to do . . .*' If they'd not followed the sun to Mecca they would have perished, His hand was upon them, He'd rewarded them with hope. '*Oh would that you know what the day of judgement is . . .*'

Justice used the plastic fence to drag himself to his feet. Even though he was standing on the pipe, it was so far beneath the water that he was submerged up to his knees.

There was shouting and sobbing. 'Move round . . . keep moving round.' They were all bunched up and needed to spread the weight.

'What do we do without a boat?' Godwin kept repeating.

'They will send us a boat,' someone shouted.

'They will leave us here and drive away,' said another.

'When they reach land they will tell the police and someone will come.'

'They must be quick,' said Hong Kong. 'Whilst it is sinking we cannot wait for the dark.'

'. . . and there was space,' shouted Godwin. 'There was space for a hundred people.'

Justice had one arm looped over the fence and was trying to pull his trousers up with the other. 'They are scared,' he said. 'A lot of black men shouting at them. They think we are pirates.'

He could see now that the pipe didn't run straight but instead formed a giant circle, so that if he edged along, he would eventually arrive back where he began. It was vast. Had it been on land it would have taken him more than a minute to run around. Strapped to the inside of the pipe was another one, the same size, which ran in parallel and meant Justice could put one foot on each to aid his balance.

'Oil,' he said.

Hong Kong was standing beside him. 'If it's oil,' he replied, 'where's it going to?'

Both pipes were narrow as mango trees but although they felt firm to the touch, when the sea moved through, they bent according to the shape of the waves. A succession of steep peaks made the whole structure writhe so that parts of it were high in the air, whilst others were swamped. And it didn't remain in the shape of a circle. It yielded with the currents so that the far side was pushed closer, then pulled away, tight like a whistling mouth, then stretched so far the plastic groaned with the effort. The fence followed the length of the structure. It was held in place by blue plastic brackets which clamped the two pipes together and then rose in a slender arm to support the yellow handrail. Without it they wouldn't have been able to stand.

'Maybe somewhere near the bottom where we can't see,' said Justice. 'The television shows it. Drilling. The oil goes to Europe.'

Hong Kong was leaning over the rail, 'If it reaches down to the floor then the water can't be deep.'

'Maybe it's as high as a house,' said Justice. 'Something like that. Maybe more. Maybe as high as ten people.'

The men had pushed along from where they first landed but not too far. They still only occupied a third of the circle. Even those who'd managed to leap straight onto it were soaked. None had landed on their feet but bent across it like they'd fallen on a sturdy branch. Now they were up, every one of them with both hands holding the yellow rail. The circle was distorted so that the area they were standing on, closest to the metal boat, was pulled outwards around where the ropes were attached.

'One . . . two . . . three . . .,' Godwin was pointing at them. 'Four, five,' Hong Kong, and then Justice, '. . . eight . . . nine.' Uncle was in a bad way, hanging motionless over the rail. '. . . thirteen . . .,' silent boy, then Daniel and AK. Godwin was calling out the numbers, the rest were following his finger around the pipe. 'Twenty-one . . . twenty-two,' Atiku in his designer cream jacket, bent double. '. . . twenty-six.' Godwin stopped. He'd come to the end of the line. There were twenty-six of them. They were one short. The pipe rose and fell in the water. The wind cleared the last warmth from the evening air.

'Where's John Gabriel?' a shout went up. They were spread over such a distance, the message had to be passed down the line.

'He's here, John is next to me.'

'What about Joshua?' It was difficult to see who was who.

'Joshua!' He lifted his head and acknowledged them with a nod.

Godwin began again, this time calling out each name as he went. They counted with him. He was halfway through when the interruptions began. 'You,' they cried. He carried on. 'You!' Twenty-six again. One of them must have been trapped in the boat. 'You!' several of them were shouting at him now, and pointing. 'You, you didn't count yourself.'

Godwin shut his eyes and wept. When he was a child, at the bungalow with the tiled hallway and the framed photos, he didn't cry when his mother left him by himself, only when she returned.

For a while there was debris on the surface: shoes, empty water bottles, jerrycans all drifting on the current. A couple of plastic bags became snagged against the pipe, then a wave freed them, and they slid away with the rest. The warm clothes they'd removed in the heat, coats and jumpers which they'd used as blankets at night, they'd gone down with the boat.

Now the men had only what they stood in. For Justice it was the tangerine T-shirt from the Medina and his red track suit bottoms which had now ballooned into pantaloons. He checked for the items hidden inside. The chip from his mobile phone was still there, zipped into a small pocket in the lining. Loose in another was a handful of cola nuts. Tucked into his waistband, his black baseball cap. And down the back of his underpants, a small cream brick of sodden paper, bound in brown leather – his Koran.

The metal boat was to his rear. He twisted himself round, keeping both hands on the rail, and shouted. 'Our boat has gone. We cannot move.'

Others joined in. 'No boat . . . no boat . . . the sea will take us.'

But the Europeans were far away. Between the pipe and the metal boat the waves were breaking white and the wind carried their voices back to them. It was stronger than it had been, licking the spindrift into a fine spray so that Justice could taste it on his tongue. The umbilical chord attaching them to the boat had sagged beneath the water and vanished. Justice followed the line and saw that it emerged again just beneath the stern, rising sharply from the water up into the crane. He could make out the Europeans, standing on the deck, watching. Next time he looked, they'd gone.

The sky to the west was pink now, and to the east the light had almost died. Justice's T-shirt stuck against his skin. A warm stream spread down the inside of his thigh. At first it wasn't unpleasant but it quickly turned cold and began to itch and sting. The sea broke against the pipe, jetting up their legs and backs, thrown so high it came down on them like freezing rain. Godwin was one of the few wearing a coat. It felt heavy but he found a damp warmth inside it, and the hood protected him from the worst of the spray.

The circle of water in the middle was calmer, the waves unable to pass through. It was also a different colour. On the outside, between the streaks of foam, the sea was dark, almost black in places. Inside it appeared menthol blue.

'There are bubbles,' said Hong Kong.

Justice saw that beneath the surface were thousands of them, rising slowly in slender threads, like the water was fizzing. 'Maybe equipment,' he said. 'From the pipes.' He lowered himself carefully and dipped in his hand. 'The same, not hot.'

When night fell, it seemed less dark than in Effiakuma. The sea captured the white light of the moon and reflected it back, so that the crests of the waves shivered with icy luminescence. The air tasted sharp, freshly washed as though after rain, but it carried within it a kind of glaze so that the men furthest along appeared to blur slightly around the edges. Even in the troughs and folds, and beneath the chilly shadow of the boat there was a silver darkness. The water in the middle responded differently, glowing as if it was lit from beneath.

That was where the noise first came from. Justice heard it too. A loud slap followed by a whoosh. At first he thought someone had fallen in but the sound was too far away. 'There,' someone shouted. 'Again, it happened again.' But there was no evidence of change. The waves continued slipping through, larger now but still unbroken.

Justice crouched and scooped a handful of water. He sucked a little into his mouth and spat it behind him. There were lights in the windows of the metal tower, soft, like a dying fire. Beyond, he saw nothing until the edge of the sky, where the low-lying stars merged with the icy crests. He thought he saw red and green lights but when he looked again they'd gone. Justice lowered himself slowly for more water, taking care not to change the position of his feet. He kept his back straight and rested his buttocks on his ankles. His other hand never left the rail. In all this vastness there was no space to move. It wasn't until he was upright again, hunched over the handrail, that he dared wash his hands and forearms, and then three times his face and scalp.

When he'd finished praying, he saw that some of the men had discovered ropes wrapped at intervals around the pipe. The ropes were binding something to its underside but the loose ends stretched away in the direction of the current. It was what Justice had clung to when they first arrived. One man fished a piece out and attempted to untie it, but it was attached firmly beneath the water. He drew the spare length around the handrail and threaded it around his waist, pulling it tightly, under the rail, over the rail, round again, and finishing with a knot. Others followed suit, lashing their bodies to the structure. Some of them were just silhouettes, hooded figures tied up in the dark.

'Uncle is quiet. His belly is big and his legs are weak,' said Justice. There was no rope near to Uncle and he was slumped over the rail, rocking with the motion of the waves.

'He is old,' said Hong Kong. 'Maybe sixty.'

'No he's forty, but still too old. Why is he here when he has a family at home?'

'His heart will be tired.'

'It is not easy for him,' agreed Justice. 'He will be the first to die.'

'What about Atiku?'

Atiku had handed his belt over to the Libyans and now his jeans were hanging around his knees. He'd left them there. His designer jacket was zipped to the collar and beneath it his soggy underpants gaped open at the front.

'He looks like a boxer,' said Justice. 'Like he's been hit hard.'

Atiku was bent double over the rail. Whenever he tried to straighten up, he began retching into the water.

'Perhaps it's the smell of salt,' said Hong Kong.

Justice felt in his pocket. 'Give him this,' he shouted, and passed a cola nut along the line.

He chewed one himself and offered another to Hong Kong. 'Against everything,' he said.

'There. It was in the water again,' one of the men on the far side of the pipe was gesticulating wildly. 'There. Black. Like a man.' The others followed his finger and saw a streak of foam on the surface. It moved swiftly across the circle and faded so that Justice wasn't sure it had been there at all.

'What is it?' asked Hong Kong.

'Do you think I know about the sea?' replied Justice.

'You said you'd swum before.'

'No, I've visited the sea before. When I was fifteen. That's all. I didn't swim. Only fish can swim.'

Hong Kong waited. 'Was it like this?'

'No, it was fine. A friend took me. We played football for a while. Then I went in the water to cool down.'

'Did you see fish?'

'No, no fish. I wasn't born near the sea. If you're not born near the sea, the sea doesn't know you and the sea can take you.'

'Over there. I saw it,' it was John Gabriel this time, the Nigerian who'd edged furthest around the pipe. 'Search yourselves,' he shouted. 'Someone is causing this. Someone has bad juju.'

John Gabriel wore a cream-coloured crucifix around his neck and had tribal scars on either cheek. His neat green polo shirt was hanging low with the weight of water. He was one of the few who hadn't yet cried. John was defiant. He'd already lost everything, long before he boarded the boat.

'Throw it in the water. It is bringing evil.' Some of them freed a hand and began feeling inside their pockets. A coin, a stone, a piece of animal skin, anything could be contaminated.

'They know it is here. That is why they have come.'

A charm intended to bring luck, that was the most likely cause. An amulet from a fetish priest who'd chanted and doused it with juices. Or maybe words and symbols scribbled on a piece of paper, a cipher to the spirit world. The guides used them to summon the desert jinn and then listened for their voices in the wind. But juju was unpredictable. Even the most reliable practitioners could misjudge the spirits. Evil could disguise itself as good. Good juju could turn to bad.

'Why did you do this? There should be no juju here. Only God can save us.'

Justice didn't search. He knew already what was in his pockets. Still thrust down his underpants was his Koran, saturated now, but its presence was comforting. 'The Koran can't sink,' thought Justice, 'and whilst it's with me, neither can I.' He didn't mention it to the others. Godwin thought maybe the culprit had swallowed the juju. Even if it was inside someone's belly it could still do its work. He examined their faces and saw all had turned to white. Red lips on white skin, sparkling in the moonlight. They peeped from beneath hoods and stared blankly into the circle, each of them rising gently into the night sky, and then descending again, until their feet vanished beneath the waves.

Justice had white arms and his hair was sprinkled with silver. Is this what happens on the sea? Is this the punishment for wanting what they have? He felt his face. It was crisp around the brow and the sides of his nose. When he brushed, white powder appeared on the tips of his fingers. He rubbed some more and worried that his face was coming away. White on his hands and behind his nails. He stuck out his tongue and licked it. Salt. They were covered in crystals of salt.

'Throw the juju into the sea,' John was shouting. 'Then the evil will go away.' But the white faces had nothing to offer and the evil remained.

Next time Justice turned around, the men were back on the deck of the big boat. He could see the amber dots of cigarettes but other than that only their coats were visible, lit yellow, like they were filled with electricity. Their legs and heads were in darkness, so when they moved it seemed the coats were floating in the air. He watched them for a while, until the bodiless jackets drifted back inside.

Justice hadn't felt cold like this before. In the desert at night they were always on the move, and if the wind blew, there were rocks or caves to hide in. Here it was the wet, the constant spray, which gave the windy night its teeth. The drops had fallen soft and glutinous once. Justice remembered he and Bakia, on a borrowed bike, racing along roads smooth as glass, water jetting up Justice's back. They'd found a valley with begonia and red ginger where the forest arched high above and sat inhaling sweet almond whilst the sky changed colour through the dripping palms. Bakia had chosen the long way home, splashing through puddles and fresh streams, shielding his eyes from the spray, and they'd carried on racing, until their clothes had fluttered dry in the sultry afternoon.

This sea wind lifted no moisture. It was cold and merciless, and had travelled far since the last sun. The back of Justice's neck ached with it and when he tried to talk, his teeth spoke different words, so they were lost before they even left his mouth. His feet hadn't been dry since leaving Zuwarah. He'd removed his shoes some time on the second day. They felt fat and ripe, and when he shifted his weight the blood pressed spongily against his soles. The skin around his toenails had been the first to go, bleaching white and then peeling away in painless strips. Then the cushion around the ball of his foot and the thick skin on his heel. As they'd swollen, the texture had changed to that of wet bread. There were criss-crossed indentations along the top of each foot which had itched red for a while and then he'd put them in the water. Nothing for a moment and then the memory hit him and he was back at the gravel square: belt, car aerial, belt.

Later there was more talk of the shapes. They were waiting just beneath the waves, 'Eyes like humans, bodies long and fat.' Only wickedness could live down there, things that didn't need air to breathe or light to see. They were evil spirits, looking for men with weak hearts. If they took you they'd use your body to give themselves form. That's what they were doing. Gliding beneath, waiting. The shapes were those of men they'd taken before. Evil always hides from light. It gathers in holes in trees and window-less cells, beneath tarpaulin sheets and secret shelters on the beach. Sometimes it creeps into huts and enters the bodies of those still alive, those who open themselves to it, who invite it in. It's always hungry for human form.

That night the twenty-seven men were on their guard. Few of them slept and those who did found no real rest. The weather worsened, so that the waves rolled in at waist height and the structure struggled. It seemed the pipe was trying to break free from its bindings. The brackets creaked against the plastic with such force they could feel the vibra-tions beneath their feet. Every few seconds another part would catch awkwardly and the sound would come again, moaning from across the other side of the circle.

The eerie sound was all that came from the pipe, the men themselves were silent. Justice folded his arms on the rail to create a cradle for his head whilst keeping a tight grip with both hands. Where are the muscles in the fingers? Can they stay tight when the head's asleep? Keep the question there, don't let it slip, the question is the muscles not the sleep; from the tips of the fingers to the tension in the wrist, keep the question there. The cheek gets warm when it's like this, lying against skin and the breath gathers in the pocket inside the elbow, meaty but warm. It comes in cold but goes out warm and there's enough to heat the skin at the tip of the nose and the inside of the nostrils. The muscles though, in the fingers, they have to stay tight. And the muscles in the forearms too, they seem to be connected. But where does the meat come from? The last meat was at the tin huts, just after the call. It was goat, from the fire, which warmed his face as he leaned in to stir the daggie. It's the shoulders though, the shoulders seem to take the tension, because the back has to be ready for the waves. And the legs of course, but there's nothing that can be done about the legs. The question is whether the head can switch off, just for a while, and the body can look after itself. Justice drifted for a while and then someone shouted that boats were approaching from behind.

He turned and saw two of them, cutting through the waves, white water pluming high along their sides. They were lit red and green, with a white light high above which threw a halo onto the sea around them.

'Praise our Maker,' said Godwin. 'He answered our prayers.' There was shouting and some nervous laughter.

'European,' said Justice. 'I can see the writing on the front. It will be fine.'

The boats were metal like the big ship, only smaller, so that they moved with the waves. There were turrets at the front, with rows of high windows behind which the shapes of people could be seen. Instead of sailing straight to the pipe, they stopped and took position alongside the boat with the tattooed men. Electric yellow jackets emerged and floated around the deck for a while. Men gathered at the side of the boat closest to the bigger one.

'Come to us ... we are suffering,' someone shouted from the pipe.

'They will come to us. They need to know how we got here, that is all.'

Justice wondered which side of the pipe they would choose first. If they began at the far end, it would be a while before they'd reach him. He was anxious about climbing the metal wall. It was too high, even with ropes.

'Check you have no papers. In case there are officials,' said Hong Kong.

Yellow jackets were hanging over the rail of the big boat shouting down to the smaller one. The third boat waited at the end of the line. Godwin removed his coat and swung it around his head. It was heavy and slapped his face and shoulders. The yellow jackets drifted to the rear so that they were facing the pipe.

'We are without food and water,' Godwin bellowed. 'No one here can swim.'

The two sides watched each other across the divide and both sides saw the same: white faces plotting and full of menace. They'd heard the stories before. Why should these people be any different? It was in their blood: greed, cruelty, deceit. It had been so for generations. Drop a gold coin on the floor and they'd take it. Glance to the heavens and they'd steal the land from beneath your feet. Always trying to take something that wasn't theirs. And they were ruthless about it. They'd even kill to get their own way.

A roll of thunder emerged from beneath the water. The engines had started and the yellow jackets were retreating inside. Soon they were back behind the turret windows and the two smaller boats were on the move. The nose of the smallest bobbed forward, until it was a length in front of the other and then it peeled away to the right. Now it was side-on to the pipe. The second boat followed suit.

'They will sink before they get here,' said Godwin.

The waves were crashing high up the metal sides of the boats, hurling spray across the decks. There were cranes, smaller than on the big boat, wheel machines wrapped with metal and giant coils of rope piled high at the rear. The boats leaned so far into the water it seemed everything should slide and then they bounced back, still turning, until they were facing the way they came. The pipe waited. The water surged and the two boats began to draw away, side by side, off into the night.

Godwin hid his face, pressing it up against the rail, sliding against the plastic and the tears. He cried so hard he felt his lungs would stick flat. 'We are dying,' he shouted when he drew breath. 'We are dying.'

Then he knelt on the pipe, holding the rail with one hand. The water could take him. If it was going to happen then God should do it now. This was suffering without hope. He clenched his fist and held it in front of him as if he was praying into a microphone.

'You are killing us,' he shouted. 'Why do you do this?'

Coats and T-shirts circled their heads. There was whistling and crying and stamping of feet. The visitors had moved away quickly, white lights joining the stars. The big boat remained but its deck was now empty. The ropes still sloped steeply from its crane, vanishing into the water and then reappearing a few metres from the pipe.

'If we hold onto that and then climb up the end . . .' said Justice.

Hong Kong was shouting with the rest. 'It is too far in the water,' he said. 'We don't know where it goes beneath the waves.'

Justice saw how the white lines gently descended. They were taut and straight, so he could go a little way, holding his breath and turn around if it carried on to the bottom.

'Through many dangers, toils and snares we have already come,' Godwin was still on his knees, but chanting now, his voice thick with tears. There was a tune in there, a familiar one. ''Twas Grace that brought us safe thus far and Grace will lead us home.'

Others hummed or called out words, one at a time, always a beat behind. The sound swirled and echoed around the pipe and was carried skywards into the night. Atiku had one arm hooked over the rail and had turned to face the boat. His hand was in the air, beseeching, his head held back, silvery lines beneath his eyes and nose. Justice dipped his hand into the water and wiped away some of the itchy salt. Then there was movement on deck. The yellow jackets had returned.

'I once was lost but now am found, was blind, but now, I see . . .'

The water boiled and a metal wheel began rotating, pouring more rope into the sea. The nose of the engines grew louder and the boat began to move away, taking the light with it. Now all of them were singing, faces turned to the moon. The pipe was being left behind. When the boat had nearly doubled its distance from the castaways, it slowed and the rope came tight. The lights on the deck went out.

Chapter Ten

'Is this what happened to you when you were here? I didn't understand the moment of change or how it would happen. It was just the difference between light and dark, not a change in me, just in everything around me. I was old and with children, and I felt the warmth of the sun and it was gentle, the change was gentle, so that my muscles were loose and my God was easily in me. But now it seems it will be a fight and it shouldn't be a fight. Did you leave with such faith that you didn't steal a breath? I shouldn't need a breath; I should empty my lungs before I hit the water. And when I awake I won't sit up sharply to see in which hand the judgement has arrived. I know it will be in my right. Those who receive it in the left will go to hell. They are the ones who've been cruel, proud and arrogant. My uncle will receive it in his left hand. He worshipped a false god and tried to force me to do the same.'

'But didn't he cure people and try to end their pain?'

'That is all he knew but he didn't do it for them, he did it for himself, to make money and to exercise his small power. He invoked the spirits, not God. The jinn whispered into his soul and he grew more wicked. He had a heart that could not comprehend and eyes that could not see. Any one of the seven gates will take him.'

'But didn't he warn you not to go into the water, the day we were on the bike?'

'When he saw the sand fall to the floor he was angry that I had disobeyed him. It wasn't because he foresaw this. He had not the power for that. He made rules to test obedience, not to prevent evil. He beat me because he was cruel and proud.'

Justice felt some of the skin from his elbow come away in his hand. 'You know my uncle. He was friends with your father. You know what he did to me. You know he was unjust. I worry now because I left my brother and sister with him. I worry about how he will treat them; maybe he's punishing them to get to me. When you return that way, have you passed by his house? He used to say, "Bakia brings worry to his father," but it was your father you did it for – him and your brothers. It needed only one of you, and you were chosen. By going you hoped the rest of them could find some peace.'

Justice rubbed his elbow and some more skin slipped away leaving raw smarting pink. There were similar patches on his hands and knees. When he touched them, they felt like plastic floating on a layer of grease, itchy grease which he needed to rub away. 'Would this have happened if I had boarded a different boat, if I had delayed a day or two?

Or was it waiting whichever way I turned? Razak knew, didn't he? That's why he never came. So many times he told us stories of the dead. I could have stayed with him but I chose not to. When I overheard the man in the orange sunglasses I chose to approach him. At Zuwarah Beach I could have turned and run. God gave me options, but how could I have known what was hidden?'

'Justice, you knew. You saw what happened to me and to DMX and the body in the desert. We were all part of the same.'

Justice sobbed and his eyes stung. He wiped them against his forearm but the silver powder made it worse and his lashes stuck like they'd been frosted with grit and ice. He had left no photographs. There were no photographs. No creased images waiting in someone's pocket. No, 'Remember him, he lived here. He was a goalkeeper.' A soiled mattress, borrowed overalls, he'd hardly disturbed the dust. No, 'He built that,' or 'These are his children,' or 'That is his grave.'

'I had a brother once' Issah would say. 'He left here before he was a man. He drew Islamic slogans on the mosque wall. They've been painted over now but they were tall and flowing and people spoke of them before they prayed.' Issah had his phone number. He would call it and leave messages, one day it would go dead, but still he'd never be sure.

It was sometime in the coldest hours, the furthest from sun to sun, and the men had fallen quiet. They were draped over the rail, ropes tied tightly, others were resting their heads like drunks at a bar.

Godwin was on his knees, hands stretched out above him and hooked over the rail. The white patches on his skin had started to peel. He'd pulled them until they were bleeding. There was too much water. He needed to stand, but there was a head in his lap, Joshua's head. His arms were wrapped around Godwin's waist.

The others, he couldn't make out their features. Just shapes shining silver in the night, coats and sweaters hanging like grotesque flaps of skin, scruffy woollen hoods swinging and lifeless. Their clothes would be useful. Joshua had only a T-shirt. If he could get round there and untie them, there were jackets and trousers. The trousers would be awkward but the jackets, even if they didn't fit, they could be worn like a blanket. Some were still moving but the majority had gone. Don't look in their eyes. He'd seen them before but never touched. Choose a small one, the bigger ones will fall and might take you with them. Silent boy, he was among them, but that was just a shirt. It was only worth it for a coat.

'I don't want this. Take away my hands and let me fall.' Joshua's face had changed. It was small and creased, his eyes were tightly shut and the motion of the structure was rocking him in Godwin's lap.

Look at him, thought Godwin, he needs a blanket. But it's a walk. Atiku's still moving and it'll be a squeeze to get past. There's blood again, it's itching, but if you pull it too far then it starts to sting. 'It stings because it's killing germs.' My mum was a nurse, she knew these things, stinging is good. I could untie some of the big ones and let them go. But what happens if a boat comes, there'll be too many questions. 'What did you do with the others? Where are the bodies to bury?' I should keep them here. Think of the spirits, the bad juju, they would never leave me alone.

Suddenly the bodies came to life. There was a crash just outside the pipe and a space where one of the men had been. The rope was still knotted to the rail but the other end was beneath the surface. Everyone was alert. 'He's in . . . pull on the rope. He's dead . . . Jesus don't let him die.' They were crouching, reaching out, stretching over the water. 'Silent boy . . . it's silent boy.' The rope was taut and down beneath the pipe. The boy was in a dark patch where the moon couldn't see. 'The rope, he's still on the rope.' One of them grabbed it and hauled it up like he was standing over a well.

The body slipped out head first, gasping and coughing, and landed face down on the pipe.

Godwin was sickened. Silent boy had sat imperious on the hatch with the waves crashing around him. He'd stuck like a spider to the side of the metal boat and now he'd been in the black water and it chose to spit him out.

'If you see a crowd of people in London, even in London, a big crowd pushing along the streets with hundreds of people, not all of them are human. Some of them have been alive once but they are not alive now, isn't that right? There will always be a few. They have a human shape but are full of spirits. They were the ones with weak hearts, so weak they couldn't fight off the spirits. That's why they are no longer humans. And the sea, the sea is full of them. So, if you come here weak, or you grow weak because there is too little food or water, the spirits see that and they know they can enter.'

Layered pink climbed the eastern sky. Silver had fallen from the crests of the waves and the glow from beneath the circle had faded. The sun was too young yet to warm the air but it slid gently through the surface picking out the early sea dust and coaxing the black into bottle green. The boat was still sleeping.

Justice's feet were heavy and cracking around the soles. He'd pulled the neck of his T-shirt up over his nose so he could breathe warm air down his front. His headache seemed to be coming from the tight balls of muscle on top of his shoulders. There was some relief, he found, if he dropped his head forwards so that it was hanging between his outstretched arms. The wind needed no rest, it swirled in furious patterns, clashing banks of water white, and tossing spindrift high into the morning air. In front of them within the circle, the sea remained strangely calm.

As the sun gathered strength, it reached deeper beneath the circle, tracing the threads of white and pink as they twisted towards the surface. The glassy green retreated. The water was on the turn – first turquoise, then menthol blue as thick shafts of light sank to dizzying depths. The pipe felt narrower than it did before and more fragile. Justice was up high, peering down from the clouds as the sub-aqua landscape revealed itself for the first time.

Attached to the underside of the pipe he could see a translucent white sheet, hanging like a vast curtain and encircling the menthol blue. It breathed in and out with the current and plunged so deep it faded to gossamer before being stolen away by the dark. The sea dust streamed right through, but there were clumps of weed pinned against it. The pipe was keeping it afloat.

Then, directly beneath his feet, he saw them – dark metallic-blue shapes moving in formation. The discovery erupted round the pipe like a foghorn.

'They are longer than a human being and fatter than three,' someone screamed. 'They will eat us all.'

The shapes moved clockwise, hugging the side of the sheet, layer upon layer of them, as if they were being stirred.

'They can smell us, that's why they're here. If you touch the water they will take you.'

The procession was unbroken, fifty wide and hundreds deep. They were so plentiful, there seemed more fish than water. Occasionally one would break the spell, accelerating away from the rest, until it was close to the surface, twisting silver, flashing its spine of dragon spikes, and thrashing its lunate tail.

'The space is too small,' said Justice. 'They cannot move. They have all of the sea, but they cannot go from here to another place. They are in a trap.'

Hong Kong was leaning over the rail, cupping his hands against the reflections. 'They are watching us,' he said. 'That is why some turn onto their sides.'

Whilst he was in Accra, Justice had seen a poster advertising an old American movie. At the top was the tiny figure of a swimming woman. She was tanned, with blonde hair and appeared to be naked. Surging up towards her through the deep blue water was the bullet-shaped head of a giant fish. The most prominent feature was its mouth, corners stretched back with momentum and fury, displaying rows of shining, dagger-sharp teeth.

'They only eat you if you swim,' said Justice. 'They've shown it on television.'

The discovery prompted more shrieking at the metal boat. 'There are wild animals here,' someone bellowed. 'You must save us.'

Justice was sure they were out of earshot but could see some activity on deck. Two of the crew had begun uncoiling a length of rope and were lowering it down one side of the boat. Whatever they'd attached to the other end was just out of sight. The waves were regularly reaching their knees now, high enough for a fish to grab a man if they timed it right.

'The Europeans sent us to this place to kill us,' said Justice, his attention fixed on his feet. 'They know there are wild animals. They want us to fall in so the problem goes away. Nobody can see what they are doing. So when they have done it, they will say they saw no boat and no Africans.'

A wave surged through and Hong Kong raised himself to his tiptoes. 'The fish must be for humans to eat,' he said. 'There are so many of them. They must take them to land.'

'Maybe they are not ready yet,' said Justice. 'Maybe they want to catch more.'

They heard a motor start and saw a grey balloon boat creep cautiously from behind the stern of the metal boat more than a hundred metres away. One of the Europeans was seated at the rear, a hand resting on the engine. He headed off across the divide, the boat hugging the contours of the waves, beating a rhythmic spray high into the morning air.

'We will not all fit,' said Justice.

They watched silently as the boat approached and then came to rest near the spot where they'd capsized. The European leant over the side and peered into the water.

'Where is it?' he shouted and then moved a little further along, inspecting the underside of the pipe. 'If you've hidden it, I will find it.' He was careful not to come too close. 'The engine might still be good. Did you tie it underneath?' No one responded. 'How did you think you would get home without a boat?' He turned around and made the same checks in the other direction, crouching to get a better view. 'We watched you turn it over. You did it on purpose so that we would have to take you on board. Don't try to force us. We will not be forced.'

Then the European banked the boat around and headed for the furthest side of the net where a slim white pole rose from the handrail like an aerial. It was twice the height of a man and on top was fitted a piece of yellow plastic that looked like an upturned cup. The European pulled in alongside and leaned over the edge so that his hands were on the pipe. He freed a length of white rope, and pulled one end of it into the boat. He was tying something which seemed to be a white bag. There was a struggle as he hoisted it over the edge and lashed it to the rail beside the poll. As he passed by on his way back, he opened his mouth and pointed inside.

The bag swayed heavily like an overripe fruit. It was Moses who was closest, a shy, athletic Ghanaian. He shuffled

226

sideways, one foot sliding then the other, rail tucked deep into his waist. He didn't stop until he'd reached it. High on the deck, the crew watched. Moses wrestled with the knot for a while then slipped the handle up his arm like a satchel and headed back to the others.

First was an apple. Moses bit into it and filled his mouth before passing it on. Another one followed and another. Bite, pass it on, bite. Justice was twenty-first in line.

Next came the water. It was a litre bottle, the sort sold in supermarkets – clear, ridged plastic with a label that had slipped near the base. Justice's lips were swollen and cracked, when he touched them against the back of his hand, they left blood. The only person who'd taken liquids since they'd arrived was a boy called Red. He'd been scooping handfuls from the sea and his eyes had turned thick like glass. Moses drank and the rest watched. His head was thrown back, the bottle vertical. They leaned over, concentrating on each mouthful. More bottles followed.

Joshua hadn't spoken since begging to be pushed in. His lips hung apart, black like tar, and his shrunken face followed the action from one mouth to the next. When the bottle reached him, he hooked both elbows over the rail, took it in his hands and drank copiously, water spilling down his chin and chest. 'Here, take it.'

Godwin was next. He reached out for the waiting bottle, clasped his hand around it, but felt nothing. He wasn't sure whether it was there or not. There was weight but not texture. The plastic made a cracking noise. Godwin thought he might have gripped too tightly, he loosened his fingers and the bottle slipped right through. There were eight people after him, all still without water. The next bottle fell in the sea before it even reached Godwin. None of them made it as far as Justice.

It was late morning on the 26th May. The wind blew damp and sticky, and only vapour trails interrupted the ink-blue sky. Justice took the baseball cap from his waistband and wore it rapper-style so it threw a shadow over the back of his neck. Others began removing waterlogged coats and knee-length sweaters, hanging them to dry along the rail. Inside the net, some of the larger fish had abandoned the circling and were basking, their fins breaking the surface like giant insect wings.

'If a wave takes you and you start to fall,' said Justice. 'Jump behind, not in front. It is better to drown than be eaten.'

Every movement of the fish was scrutinised. When they drifted too close, the shouting began. 'Get back . . . Not here.' The braver ones reached out a foot and kicked the water. Sometimes a gleaming black hump emerged above the waves and the volume increased. It seemed to have an effect; the fish would sway lethargically back to the middle and take up position facing the men.

Next time Justice crouched for his ablutions, he took water from outside the circle, even though it was more effort to reach. The hat needed to come off. He'd been rotating it with the changing position of the sun. Take it off now and scoop some water, cool and refreshing. The back of his neck needed it too. Carefully though, slowly. His hands were heavy and when he caught his fingers against the pipe it felt like electricity. Just there in the tips, like something was buzzing inside. He scratched but that seemed to make it worse. It was in his lips too. He bit them, trying to squeeze the feeling away but a metallic warmth filled his mouth and he felt the cracks opening wider with his tongue. He needed to be careful. His tongue was a little larger now and when he spoke he caught it between his front teeth. He needed to keep it in but it kept squeezing out.

Not as bad as that boy over there, the one with the cream designer jacket, the one being sick. He needed a cola nut. But Justice's pockets seemed to have shrunk and he could only fit a couple of thick fingers inside. Wasn't that the phone chip, with the tape wrapped around it? Something sharp anyway. More electricity. Move gently and it goes away. They're peanuts now, all shrunken, like Joshua's head, but they still contain the medicine. Maybe give him a couple. How can he be sick when there's no water in his belly? The one who used to play football, what's his name, he always wore a woollen hat? The thing with cola nuts is that they're best eaten fresh. The pink ones especially. Once they age they turn to rubber, but if he chews hard he'll find some juice. It's not the phone chip you know. That's in the zip pocket. It's those dollars. They'll dry later. Leave them now or they'll tear. Is anyone going to help him? His head is as low as his knees. Cola nuts, those would make him better.

They shielded their eyes from the midday sun, trying to keep track of the surface fish, but the light leapt fiercely. Those who had the strength unhooked jackets and jumpers from the rail and draped them over their heads. Whenever

Justice opened his eyes, his lids seemed full of grit and even when they were shut they were weeping and crusted. Now when he listened he heard mosquitoes.

He ignored them and rotated his hat. The worst were those in Qatrun. No not there, the place before that, the police station with the insect bread. Whichever way he lay they seemed to sniff out his exposed skin: between his toes, around his waistband, even on his temples. It seemed they knew where to find the veins. At night they always seemed to circle his ears, like they were looking for a way in. The cockroaches were better – ugly but no biting.

'Boat,' someone cried.

Out in the livid distance, a single cigar-shaped boat was bouncing across the waves, nose cocked high, flumes of water churning from its rear. It was moving quickly, kicking so hard, it seemed to fly through the air. Its nose took up half of its body, black like ebony, and tapering to a sharp point. The seats were at the rear, set out in rows of three, the occupants strapped in, wearing shiny orange vests and sunglasses. One of them was on his feet, hair buffeting in the wind, gripping a steering wheel that looked like it came from a bus.

It approached from Justice's left, skipping to a halt beside the metal boat. The tattooed men appeared on deck and the two vessels fell into rhythm. Justice became tired of turning his head and rested it on the rail instead. Why was there still water coming out of him? He'd put none in. There was less of it this time, but it was still hot and stinging, and he pinched the cotton away so it trickled over his yellowing feet and away into the sea.

The next time he looked, the cigar-shaped boat was no more than ten metres away and dawdling, curiously, along the pipe. The occupants wore T-shirts and jeans beneath their shiny orange vests. They spoke little, viewing the men as if on parade, and when they reached the end, they turned and passed slowly back the same way.

The shouts, when they came, were fewer and weaker than before. 'Dying please,' or 'Here long time.' Others just mouthed and pulled faces, or pointed to themselves and then to the boat. The twenty-seven heads were at the same height as the five crewmen, so it felt as though they were almost amongst them, that the gap was narrow.

They stayed with them for a time, baseball caps pulled low, the captain twitching his wheel against the waves. But the weather was worsening, the pipe slid upwards, higher than before, drawn into banks of teetering blue. Sometimes the summits divided them, so that Justice was still climbing whilst the other side had vanished over the top. When the cigar-shaped boat had seen enough it turned, blew its engines, and set off back from where it came. The fishermen waved, and the men in orange vests waved back.

Joshua was on his feet. Last night he was ready to die. That little shrunken head with those red eyes. Half his body was underwater. Godwin had almost agreed, he'd seemed to want it so badly. Now his eyes were closed but his legs seemed strong. How had he been reborn? They must have entered him, when his heart was weak. Godwin should have searched his pockets. It was Joshua who was the disobedient one. They'd been told to throw away all their money. Now look at him. He was leaning back against one of several giant yellow tyres through which the pipe ran at intervals of ten metres. There was one directly behind Godwin. It was some kind of balloon coated in cushioned plastic. Joshua was reclining into it, like it was an armchair, feet on the pipe, hands well away from the rail.

Godwin couldn't turn to look. Only someone who was not alive would take such a risk. Joshua was waiting for the rest of them. He was in no hurry. In time, they'd fall, and then, when the job was done, he'd take off beneath the ocean.

It was Red, the sea drinker, who fell that afternoon. It had begun with lip-wetting, nothing more, just enough to stop the cracking and moisten the tongue. Justice shouted, 'God made it bitter because it is poison,' but Red ignored him. During the morning, he began swilling it around his mouth and then let a little slip down his throat. Despite the pain in his stomach, it did seem to quench his thirst. Soon though, his mouth furred up again, and there was a fierce pulse in his head. When the bottled water arrived, none made it as far as Red. He started sucking up mouthfuls of sea again and it seemed the more he drank the more he needed.

At first it had been difficult to detect a change in his behaviour. It wasn't just Red who'd fallen quiet that afternoon: the dehydration, the hunger, the exhaustion, it had silenced them all. But there were signs that Red was different. His eyes were like balls of rolling glass, and when they shouted to him, he turned and stared right through them. He began spitting out powdery phlegm and even tried to sit down, unconcerned about his legs dangling in the water. No one was watching at the moment of entry. He might have leapt, even he doesn't know. He didn't struggle to climb back and it was only because he was tied to a rope that they were able to save him. When he was back among them Red began speaking in tongues.

Godwin watched from further down the line. 'Another one,' he thought.

Just after three o'clock a plane appeared in the sky. It was lower than those they had seen before and left no stripe. Justice tried to catch the markings but they were unfamiliar, just numbers and letters. It had a swollen belly, curving steeply beneath its front, and short stubby wings with paddles like ceiling fans. Justice tried to tell them to wave their clothes but when he spoke it sounded like his mouth was full of food. He tilted himself as far back as he dared and watched the plane pass directly overhead.

'On the way to Europe,' he thought. 'For holidays.' A few minutes later it returned, passing lower this time, a flying juggernaut shaking the air.

A fine haze settled over the water that evening. The blue drained from the heavens and the air was filled with milky light. The warmth was almost gone and the wind was gathering strength. Justice's tracksuit flapped around his knees. Soggy jackets and jumpers were pulled back on. The metal boat lurched, unable to deal with the growing waves.

At 7.30 p.m. there were vibrations in the air and beneath the water. 'Thunder,' thought Justice, and it shook the net and churned the sea. New patterns appeared on the surface, foaming spirals and circular streaks. The waves were pressed flat and the spray twisted upwards. And then it emerged out of the haze – a hovering grey hulk with a single fan roaring on its back.

It manoeuvred itself until it was directly above them, buffeted by the wind, its tail swinging one way, then the other. Justice saw an opening on the side. A door had been drawn back and inside were people. It seemed to achieve some stability, still twitching, but maintaining a position directly overhead. A figure appeared and sat in the doorway, legs hanging over the edge. Then he was out, flying through the air on the end of a piece of rope or maybe he had wings. Slowly now, carefully, edging towards them, still as high as a building, but dropping all the time – any further and he'd be in the waves. But the hulk corrected itself and he was gliding towards them, twisting slowly, his boots just above their heads. Then he was down, feet on the pipe, standing among them.

The man was wearing a plastic suit and carrying orange vests with oblong patches of electric white. He released himself from the rope and it shot back up. Another man descended and landed close to Justice. The thunder eased and the machine withdrew into the night sky.

The two men were shouting and shaking them, edging nimbly around the pipe, holding people's heads and staring into their faces. 'Take it.' One of them was beside Justice offering an orange vest. He put his gloved hands on top of Justice's fingers and began to uncurl them from around the rail.

'No,' said Justice. 'Leave.' The man tried again, prising

his fingers with some force. The waves thrashed behind and Justice wasn't sure his legs could hold him.

'Quickly, it will take just a second,' the vest was next to him, and the gloved hand was back, forcing his fingers away. They were off for a moment, then in through the sleeve, and back onto the rail.

The process was slow. Some resisted so fiercely it required both men to wrestle their hands free. By 8.35 p.m., an hour after the helicopter arrived, every one of the twenty-seven was wearing a lifejacket.

It was dark now and the electric white oblongs formed an unsteady arc around the pipe. There were lights rising and falling behind them, and they saw boats, three of them, small like the one they'd boarded at Zuwarah Beach. The boats nosed up close but the waves rushed beneath them and threatened to hurl the vessels across the pipe and into the circle. The two men on the net were crouching and gesturing, reaching out for ropes.

There was a lull. One boat seized the moment, burst across the gap, turned sharply and nestled alongside. The crew reached out their arms, tugging gently at one of the migrants, encouraging him to step backwards into safety. He refused. They tried the next, lifting both of his legs in turn so he could feel the solidity of the boat, but he wouldn't allow his hands to leave the rail. Then the two men who'd dropped from the sky set to work on his fingers, but he screamed and cried until they let go.

It was dark when the warship arrived. There were bright lights shining white, green and red, and uniformed men busy on deck. The boat was longer than any Justice had

seen before, with turrets built on turrets and fenced walkways linked by flights of stairs. On its crest were aerials,
swivelling dishes and curious large white eggs.

It passed the fishing boat without pausing. 'Okay,'
shouted the two men in plastic suits. 'It's okay. Not long.'

The waves were growing. They were taller than a man,
taller than a house. Justice held on tight and dipped his
head against the wind. The ship approached on the far side,
close to John Gabriel. It slowly turned, seething the water
around it, breathing it in at the stern and blowing it out at
the bow, so that the ship moved sideways towards the net
and then sat still against it like a city block. Suddenly, the
wind dropped and the air became almost still. To either
side of the ship the waves raged as before, but everything
in its shadow fell quiet. The net settled and the water was
near calm.

A small boat moved gently behind Justice. Hands reached
out to support his legs and back, and now, finally, he let
go. There was a hard floor and booted feet. He felt the
water move beneath him and then there was a door. It was
an opening cut into the side of the warship, close to its rear.
They were alongside it, just three steps below. There were
others before him, each was passed upwards to the white
faces, and then Justice followed.

It was 9.45 p.m. Godwin was in the last boat. When they
finally passed him through the door, his legs gave way and
he found himself crawling towards the others. They were
in a group on the deck, some sitting, others lying on blue
and white blankets. The men in uniforms wore white plastic
gloves and masks over their mouths like doctors. They

brought them sheets made from metal paper: silver on one side, bronze on the other and wrapped each of them tightly inside. There was water and hot tea.

'What is this place?' the migrants asked. Some thought they might have reached land. The deck had a rough black texture, like the surface of a road. 'Is this Europe?'

Justice sat upright. 'Italy,' he said. 'Their shoulders say Italy. That is where they are from.' His feet were swollen and when he pressed, the skin turned white and only gradually regained its colour.

Godwin tried to stand to remove his wet trousers but his legs were trembling and he fell and lay on the floor, sobbing. They covered him with a blanket. For a while he was in bed at the family bungalow in Tema. Then two hands lifted him beneath the shoulders, sat him upright and gave him hot drinks.

Later they carried him, 'like a footballer', to the ship's doctor, where he was given tablets and fresh clothes – an all-in-one paper jumpsuit, designed to keep in the heat. It was white and had a hood with an elastic tie around the face. Everyone wore the same. Only Justice looked different. He insisted on wearing his black baseball cap over the top of his hood, twisted rapper-style.

That night, they slept for the first time since leaving Zuwarah. In the early hours of 27 May, Commander Davide Berna, captain of the *Orione*, received a telephone call telling him where to take them.

The sea was gentle and the sun warm. It was 8 a.m. on the Sunday morning and the *Orione* was sailing past high limestone cliffs. They'd crumbled in places and grass had sprouted on ledges and on the piles of boulders which had collected at the base. Around the next headland, the cliffs gave way to sandy coves and they could see parched farmland and narrow empty roads. After a time, the sea became busy. There were shining boats, with beds open to the sun where young women lay in their underwear. Children jumped head first from the side, splashing into the water and then climbing back on board up silver ladders. Some of the women had taken off their bras.

Justice had never known where he was heading. Not when he hid on top of the desert truck as it raced towards the Algerian border, nor when he pulled his friends through the hole in the prison wall, shivering and coughing into the Qatrun night. Even when he was waiting in Libya it was unclear: blow-torching goats' heads and eating their brains; packed into a pick-up truck with the others 'like chickens'; watching the Libyan abandon the boat and dive into the sea. In all of that, he'd never known. He was doing lampa-lampa, his journey to the Promised Land, but where it was, he didn't know.

They came upon a bay where people lounged on towels and paddled on inflatable mattresses. Beyond it was a harbour where the UN and Médecins Sans Frontières were preparing for the new arrivals. As they approached, a member of the crew addressed the twenty-seven men, and Justice finally understood.

'It's an Italian island,' the crewman said. 'They will look after you here. Its name is Lampedusa.'

Epilogue

It was whilst making a film for the BBC *Panorama* programme in the summer of 2007 that I first met Justice Amin. He was sitting in the foyer of a hostel run by the Catholic Church, just outside Naples. It was, to Western eyes at least, a grim and hopeless place occupied by drunkards and down-and-outs, and situated in an area of town long ago ghettoised by African migrants and other outcasts.

Justice was sitting away from the glare of the sun, in a gloomy corner of tropical plants, plastic and faded. Four others from the tuna net were alongside him, waiting for their evening meal. Among them Atiku, who described what had happened with exuberant gestures, showing how he'd prayed and cried, before throwing his hands to the ceiling to indicate the height of the waves. Justice watched silently from his chair, distant and suspicious.

When we finally got talking, he explained that he'd been brought up in Ghana by his uncle. He didn't say what his uncle did, or why he'd run away, all that would come later. I asked if he'd phoned his uncle to tell him he was safe. 'No,' he replied. 'My uncle is dead.' I told him I was sorry to hear that, and asked what he'd died of. Justice shook his head. 'Wickedness,' he said. 'He died of wickedness.' For a journalist, he couldn't have been more intriguing.

That meeting took place about a month after the men were rescued. They were discovered ninety miles north of Libya, eighty miles south of Lampedusa, hanging onto a tuna net which was being pulled by a Maltese tug. The crew of the tug had refused to take them on board, 'in case they turned violent and killed everyone.' The boss, who was directing operations from Malta, says they had more than a million dollars of tuna in the net, and taking the men back to land would have meant sacrificing the entire catch, without any hope of compensation.

They were rescued by the Italian warship, the *Orione*. Its captain, Commander Davide Berna, says when he arrived on the scene, sea conditions were deteriorating rapidly and the men were so weak within 3–4 hours he believes all would have perished. It was he who took them to Lampedusa.

During the summer, the island's tiny harbour is transformed into a busy field hospital. Men sit on the quayside, bewildered and haunted. There are women carrying screaming babies, children without parents, pregnant mothers, all part of the human tide which gathers and builds with each passing year. Justice and the others joined them, and were transferred to the island's holding centre where they were given medical attention and washed and fed before being flown to mainland Italy.

Such was the ordeal they'd endured, the authorities decided to let them stay, at least for a year. All were given train tickets to a city of their choice, and rushed off to Venice, Rome and Naples to begin their new lives.

It wasn't long before reality crashed in. They were homeless, jobless migrants. They couldn't speak the language. They knew no one, had no connections. They were spectators staring out from behind the gates of charity hostels or worse still, from the dark corners of railway stations where they'd bedded down for the night. They were in Europe, but not of it.

As I write this, two years after their arrival, only a handful have found work. Mostly it's been shifts in factories, short-term manual jobs, heavy labour – the sort left over when everything else is gone. None I've spoken to have sent money home. Their wages barely cover their rent. At least though they've found some purpose, some hope, the briefest taste of milk and honey. The vast majority have remained jobless. They've melted away into Europe's invisible underclass, roaming from one country to the next in search of work, begging and scavenging, sleeping rough – a wretched existence some have described as worse than what they left behind.

Justice Amin

Justice left the Catholic mission in Naples in the autumn of 2007 and headed for the town of Breno, high in the Italian Alps. He stayed in a refugee centre there, a well-run modern building in a smart residential area of town, with views over snow-capped peaks and dramatic valleys. I visited him that winter, and commented how beautiful it was. 'I am not here on holiday, Mr Paul,' he said. 'I am here to work.' He still had with him his small leather bound Koran. 'Lick it,' he said, peeling open a random page, and I could taste the sea.

Each morning he rose at 5 a.m. for prayers, then made his way to the job centre. After two months without success, he decided to move south to a larger city. It's a mysterious gift Justice has, that wherever he travels he seems to discover Ghanaians willing to help. Whether he approaches them in the street or a station, or harvests their details from migrants who've passed that way before, he sweeps them along with his charm and quiet dignity, and adds them to a network of contacts which seems to spread over most of Italy and beyond. It was whilst staying with friends in the northern city of Cremona, that his determination to find work eventually paid off. Early one morning in May 2008, I received a telephone call from the back of a speeding taxi: Justice had an interview at a carpet factory. So excited was the woman from the job centre, she'd gone with him. Somehow he managed to convince the factory managers he'd operated the machines before, and was given the job. Three days later, the machine broke and Justice was laid off.

Then, towards the end of May 2008, there was a breakthrough. He appeared on Italian television to mark the first anniversary of the rescue from the tuna net. Seated beside him was the tireless human rights worker Laura Boldrini from the UN refugee agency, the UNHCR. Justice spoke in his limited Italian, and between them they outlined the difficulties African migrants experience once they've arrived in Italy. After the broadcast, there was a phone call from Sardinia. Justice was offered a job on a building site. Within a couple of weeks he'd caught a boat, a large metal one this time, to the town of Olbia on the north coast. When I visited him he proudly declared himself 'the only Ghanaian on the island,' and stayed for three months before the work finished.

Now he's back in northern Italy, living in Reggia Emilia with a Ghanaian couple. He attends the job centre every morning but is, at the moment, without work. Nevertheless, he seems happy to stay in Italy for a while. He still talks about coming to the UK, but would need more paperwork. Eventually he wants to return to Ghana to marry and have children.

For Justice, Europe was never an end in itself, it was part of a simple desire to improve his life. Whether or not he succeeds is still very much in the balance.

In the autumn of 2008 I visited Ghana to see the town where he grew up, and find out more about his Uncle Ibrahim. I was led into an overgrown graveyard in the forest outside Effiakuma. The light was fading, and the path was difficult to follow. We came to a clearing where there was a single tall tree. Beneath it was a mound of earth with a branch to mark its place. 'We were pleased when he died,' said one of the guides. 'He was a bad man.'

Uncle Ibrahim fell ill in May 2007, the same month Justice

set sail from Zuwarah Beach. It was only when he arrived in Europe that he learned of his uncle's death. As he once said to his friend and teacher, Musah, 'One of us will have to die for me to be free.'

Godwin Akuamoah

Godwin spent his first few months in Europe staying at a hostel near Venice. It's a former army camp used to house drug addicts, alcoholics and migrants. They live in wooden chalets hidden away in the forest – pleasant enough – but the city and jobs are a long bus journey away.

In the summer of 2007 I sat with him in the hostel's canteen, drinking coffee and eating spaghetti. He asked me to describe Britain and then followed me round for the rest of the day, offering to carry bags or to help with the filming equipment. He was so innocent, so humble and gently needy I couldn't imagine how he'd survive without an adult to guide him. It was only later, in a phone call, that I discovered what had happened to his parents.

Godwin left the hostel after a few months, and travelled to the town of Pordenone in northeast Italy. There he met a Ghanaian who offered him a place to stay. He's still there today. In the evenings he eats at a charity-run hostel, and sometimes visits another survivor from the tuna net, Husseini Adams, the silent boy who sat on the hatch. Godwin no longer thinks he's a witch.

Every Sunday he attends the local church, and sometimes, to help lift his mood, he writes hymns. When he was struggling to describe his mother's shooting to me over the phone, he sang this:

'In a believer's ear, it soothes his sorrows,
  heals his wounds and drives away his fear.
Dear name, the rock on which I build my child and
    hiding place,
My never-failing treasury filled with boundless stores
    of grace.
Jesus, my shepherd, saviour, friend, my prophet, priest
    and king.
My Lord, my life, my way, my end.
Accept the praise I bring.'

One night in October 2008 he phoned me several times, terrified that the people who'd killed his mother had traced him to Italy and were about to do the same to him. Around the same time he was treated in hospital for stress.

Unlike Justice, Godwin never wants to return to Africa. 'I have nothing there,' he says. 'I am a stranger to the place.'

Despite visiting the job centre almost every day, Godwin has never found work.

Atiku

Atiku was the most unpredictable and difficult to engage with. In the beginning he was self-confident, articulate and almost vibrating with energy. He travelled to Naples with Justice, and stayed in the Catholic mission there, but soon became restless, and dashed off northwards, alone and without a plan. He ended up sleeping at the railway station in Brescia, until a Ghanaian spotted him and took pity. Atiku slept on the man's floor for a while, but the arrangement clearly couldn't last. I visited him there in the autumn of 2007. He was terrified he'd end up back on the streets, and as a result, oscillated from taciturn silence to ranting frustration.

The others lost contact with him for several months after that. Then in the summer of 2008 he phoned Justice and said he'd been living in Sweden. It's understood he has found work there, and intends to stay.

Ibrahim Musah – Justice's friend and Arabic teacher

Musah still lives in Effiakuma, buzzing around on his cream-coloured scooter, stopping to chat with everyone he meets. In the autumn of 2008 we were riding in the back of a taxi when he delivered a bombshell. He was listing the languages he could speak, 'Arabic and English,' he said. 'Twe and Hausa. Oh, and a little Italian.' Italian? I was surprised, and pressed him to explain.

One morning in 1995, when Musah was seventeen years old, he left his mother's home in Effiakuma to earn money for his education. He set off northwards, across the Sahara, and headed for the Libyan coast. There he fell into the hands of people-smugglers and ended up boarding a small boat for Europe with around fifty others. Between them they had five life jackets.

When they ran out of food, a Nigerian man shouted to

him, 'Hey Musah do you have some Gari?' and Musah shared some of his sweet ginger pickle. After six days a storm hit. Their boat filled with water and capsized. As it did so, the Nigerian threw Musah a lifejacket. That's how he survived. A life for a piece of pickle. The rest died.

After his rescue, he spent several months in Italy, but became ill and was forced to return home. He bought a place on a small overcrowded boat organised by people-smugglers, this time heading for Africa.

I was speechless. Musah had never told anyone before, apart from his mother. 'It's not unusual,' he said. 'Five people left from here last week to do the same.'

Razak 'from the butchering shops of Gurji'

In the winter of 2008 Razak left Libya and made the two-thousand-mile journey back home to Ghana. To the delight of his mother, he married a local girl and stuck around for a while. But their finances were tight. It was his mother who suggested he return to Libya, and he did so early in 2009.

Now he's back in Gurji, working in the meat market, friend and confidante to the newcomers. He says his wife will join him soon, making the same dangerous journey across the Sahara. Then they plan to have children.

Razak isn't sure how long they'll stay in Libya. He's thirty-nine now, and working six days a week in the dark and the blood. Whatever happens, he's lost so many friends to lampa-lampa, he's adamant he'll never try it himself.

*

In 2008 the UNCHR suggested 31,043 people successfully crossed the Mediterranean from Libya to Lampedusa, not far short of a hundred a day. In one three-day period alone, over Christmas 2008, the number of arrivals approached 2,000.

The UN puts fatalities at 525, based on the number of bodies found, reports in the media and information gleaned from survivors in Lampedusa but the true number is obscured by the secrecy of the departures. The International Organisation for Migration, the IOM, estimates the number of deaths closer to 2,000, based on findings from Libya, Malta, Tunisia and Italy but even these figures are thought to be far short of the actual total. Then there are those unknown numbers who die in the desert.

Today the IOM estimates there are between 750,000 and a million African migrants waiting on the Libyan coast for their chance to try lampa-lampa.

Acknowledgements

I wish to thank my wife, Flavia, who put up with my long-absences, listened patiently deep into the night, and without whose constant encouragement the story would not have been told.

Elena Cosentino from the BBC managed to track down Justice and the others in the first place. Her fierce energy and gentle compassion helped me maintain mine. At the BBC, I need to thank Frank Simmonds who oversaw all the *Panorama* programmes I made on the subject and who checked the manuscript with the assidious attention to detail for which he is legendary. I also thank the *Panorama* editor Sandy Smith who had the vision to commission the story for the BBC and my producer Howard Bradburn, who covered much of the journey with me and has the rare gift of finding a decent wine in the most unlikely of countries. Thanks to Laura Boldrini at the UNHCR. Her dedication to refugees, both political and economic is, quite simply, humbling. So too is that of Laurence Hart from the IOM, whose overview of the route was crucial. In Libya, I could not have operated without the help and insight of the BBC's Rana Jawad. In Ghana, Anny Osabutey, took me to Justice's home, and charmed the entire neighbourhood. In Valetta, Major Ivan M. Consiglio was available night and day for instant comment on the Maltese perspective. I would have known nothing of sea conditions without the help of Richard Stretch from the Met Office, and nothing of sea survival without Dr Frank Golden and Dr Michael Tipton whose book *Essentials of Sea Survival* was always close to hand. Captain Keith Hopkins from the Warsash Maritime Academy gave me important advice about the performance of Justice's boat.

Finally, I and Justice would like to thank Commander Davide Berna. He was the captain of the Italian warship which rescued the men. Without his professionalism, and that of his crew, the ending could have been very different.